SNOWBIRD

The Story of Anne Murray

D1196210

Quarry Press Music Books

Neil Young: Don't Be Denied
by JOHN EINARSON

Magic Carpet Ride: The Autobiography of John Kay & Steppenwolf
by JOHN KAY and JOHN EINARSON

American Woman: The Story of The Guess Who
by JOHN EINARSON

Superman's Song: The Story of Crash Test Dummies
by STEPHEN OSTICK

Encyclopedia of Canadian Rock, Pop & Folk Music
by RICK JACKSON

Encyclopedia of Canadian Country Music
by RICK JACKSON

Oh What a Feeling: A Vital History of Canadian Music
by MARTIN MELHUISH

Some Day Soon: Profiles of Canadian Songwriters
by DOUGLAS FETHERLING

Snowbird

The Story of Anne Murray

by
BARRY GRILLS

Quarry Press

~√

For my brother, Richard

Copyright © Barry Grills, 1996.

The publisher gratefully acknowledges the support of
The Canada Council, Ontario Arts Council,
and Department of Canadian Heritage.

Many of the photographs in this book were issued for publicity
purposes by CBC-TV, Capitol Records, EMI, and CARAS, while
others were supplied by sources who wish to remain anonymous.

The cover image is a reproduction of the Capitol-EMI publicity
sheet for SOMETHING TO TALK ABOUT.

Canadian Cataloguing in Publication Data

Grills, Barry
    Snowbird : the story of Anne Murray

Includes discography.
ISBN 1-55082-153-9

    1. Murray, Anne 2. Singers--Canada--Biography.
I. Title

ML420.M86G75   1995   782.42164'092   C95-900876-4

Printed and bound in Canada by Best Book Manufacturers,
Toronto, Ontario.

Published by Quarry Press,
P.O. Box 1061, Kingston, Ontario K7L 4Y5.

CONTENTS

Anne Murray poses for this publicity portrait as host of the 1996 Juno Awards.

Photo – George Whiteside

YOUR HOST

ANNE MURRAY

FOREWORD

When Anne Murray took the stage to host the 1996 Juno Awards in Toronto in March, she was nearly fifty-one years old. Her gait was familiar to the Canadians watching the telecast, not only because it retains a trace of the gym teacher she once was, but because it has, along with everything else about Anne Murray, infiltrated our consciousness. There are those who claim she is an institution, our ambassador to the world, even a reflection of the Canadian identity. But that's not why she seems so familiar. Not really. Rather it's just that we realized, as we have so many times before, that Anne Murray has been absorbed into our musical sense like no-one ever has before. Such has been the woman's power and influence on us that we don't even have to be a dedicated fan to feel that we know her and her music intimately. The many songs and the many televised appearances have somehow become part of our collective consciousness. You recognize each tune, even if you can't remember where you heard it before. She looks as familiar as your sister, although you don't quite remember why.

At fifty, she's permitted her hair to be gray, not blonde anymore. On Juno night, she seemed mature, although we all found ourselves flashing back to when she was much younger, believing yet again that we thought we know this woman, she's become so much a part of us. We probably cast a jaundiced eye on her green outfit, an ensemble designed specifically for the occasion, yet we winced less because Anne Murray has worn some pretty awe and puzzle-inspiring outfits in the past than because we're Canadians and see high fashion as kind of a delicate migraine headache, an interruption in our perpetual state of practical good health.

All of this made her seem familiar but we still don't know her. We just think we know our performers and entertainers, its our proprietary prerogative. Thinking we know the person and not truly knowing her is as true of Anne Murray as it is of anyone in the entertainment business. Probably even more so.

Because Anne Murray has always been an enigma. "Elusive" was the word writer David Livingstone used in his 1981 book *Anne Murray: The Story So Far*. Her long career has revealed a variety of personalities, some of them inconsistent with one another. She has approached stardom reluctantly, then chased after it voraciously. She has been barefoot and easy, then glitzy and tough. She has sometimes said one thing, then done another. She has ducked dozens of opportunities, then manipulated dozens more. She has been small town and she has been world capitol.

But on Juno night, when she sang, no matter all the conflicting things she has been, she was familiar to the point where public ownership of her cannot be questioned. We know instantly it is Anne Murray and that it seems she has always been a musical star, *our* musical star. And some of us are convinced we knew that this would happen, knew it all along, even way back then when her musical story was just beginning.

I remember the first time I personally heard of Anne Murray. Not on television, not on radio, but in the offices of Capitol Records. It was way back then, virtually at the beginning. That particular "then" when everyone seemed so much younger and fresher than they do now. Like your clothes fit so much better. Like you shine. Like even tragedy will end up humorous.

Those were heady musical days. The turbulent 1960s had now concluded, albeit only technically. I say technically because the equally turbulent first half of the 1970s was just underway. Music in virtually every genre had become the weapon in a skirmish between a perceived cultural underground and an opposing cultural mainstream. As a musical audience, split between AM and

FM radio, we tended to dismiss the creativity of the opposing side as trash. Those of us who liked the apparently more revolutionary underground groups and artists had a tendency to make light of the mainstream music, describing it as commercial or bubblegum. (Murray herself would battle the notion of what was "hip" and what was not, resenting at times her placement in the battleground.) At the time, it never entered our minds to consider that, first of all, all music is commercial, that in modern times music is a high-powered business of agents, managers, accountants, grease, and publicity, or that music which was commercial did not automatically condemn it to creative inadequacy. Those who enjoyed the mainstream artists had a tendency to believe, if they did not dismiss heavier rock and blues as empty anarchy, that alternative underground music was the voice of a deeply troubled social consciousness masquerading as legitimate rebellion.

It was also the historic era in which the CRTC (Canadian Radio-Television Commission) had come up with its Canadian content regulations. Here, there was rejoicing in both camps. Previous to this, although some Canadian music had managed to compete well in the world marketplace, most of it did not receive much airplay, regardless of quality, and consequently was not deemed economically viable. The new regulations quite literally forced radio stations to play Canadian music 30 percent of the time and, as this would enhance sales of Canadian music and at times reverse this economic disadvantage, the stage was set for a much-deserved Canadian musical renaissance.

By 1970, people who knew of Anne Murray's rich, contralto voice, knew her either through the Maritimes-based CBC production *Singalong Jubilee*, or had purchased her first album on Canadian label Arc which had sold moderately well. In my own case, a supporter at the time of underground music, I might never have heard of her in those early days except that I too was involved in a fledgling way in the music business and was intent on garnering a record contract for my brother and his rock group of the time, Bill the Lizard. And so, not once had I watched *Singalong Jubilee*, not once had I tuned in the country side of music. Instead, I encountered Anne Murray as an entity, the great Maritime hope, in the Canadian offices of Capitol Records.

I had driven to Toronto to speak to record companies which, at the time, were being deluged with new acts. Certainly opportunities seemed more promising in view of the CRTC regulations. Word was that international record companies with offices in Canada were looking for Canadian performers, to take advantage of that aforementioned potential for economic viability. It was also said that independent Canadian recording was going to move out of its slipshod network of garages and basements to take on the big guys. Was this not a tremendous opportunity for talented musicians to record? Ultimately we dealt with MCA in Toronto, then Warner Bros., then Polydor. But one of the first stops that summer was Capital Records.

Hence my first encounter with Anne Murray, a vocal performer who would ultimately take home more musical awards and related honors than she could carry, who would dazzle millions with her rich, vibrant voice, who would crack that great cultural court, the United States, on which Canadians tend to depend for our international cultural credibility, who would become one of this country's most famous Canadians and who would, more than 25 years later, remain a certifiable international musical superstar.

I do not remember the name of the man in whose office I pitched my brother's group. I do not even recall what he looked like. For all I know, it might have been Paul White, the A & R man, jack of all trades, producer and designer of albums like THE HITS OF GERRY AND THE PACEMAKERS, who signed Anne Murray and ultimately resided with Balmur Ltd., Murray's management company. But mostly I remember *the presence* of Anne Murray who was jammed inside this big city office in the form of promotional materials, photographs, and record album jackets. And the strange thing is, if Anne's history had developed entirely differently, if she had not amassed the musical achievements she did, I would still remember her to this day. And I don't even know why. Except that perhaps some people have a mysterious quality, a drive, perhaps even a predestined script, a potential for *familiarity* which is going to rocket them into the domain we call "success in your chosen field." I'm not saying I saw all of this that day in a small office at Capital Records. I *am* saying, however, that

I *think* I did, and that the vast nature of Anne Murray's achievements as a vocalist, performer, personality, and Canadian failed forever to surprise me as each year gained her more and more appreciation by audiences around the world. So I think I saw something. I think I knew. I think you have it or you don't. And I think that indefinable *it* which some people possess occasionally defies definition, especially when it has an almost preordained connotation. Call it talent, call it drive, call it a gift for developing a career, call it whatever you want. Just make sure to call it more than luck or timing or chance.

It's a gift, this ability to enthral musically. And if I noticed it in 1970 in the presence of mere photographs and the enthusiastic hype of an unnamed record executive, Paul White or not, there are those who knew her intimately when she was young who must have recognized it even more profoundly.

A great deal has happened in Anne Murray's life since 1970. Much of it happened before that year and much of it remains to happen in the years which lie ahead.

The management at Balmur Ltd., Anne Murray's company, as management so frequently does, when someone proposes a biography of their talent, informed me that "Ms. Murray will not co-operate with any biographer at this stage of her career." The letter saying so was signed by then managing director J. Lyman MacInnis who filled the management breach for less than a year before Bruce Allen took over, on the heels of the tragic death from cancer of Leonard Rambeau, Anne Murray's manager for so many years. Such points of view are common, especially from management. And not all people who reach the pinnacles of fame or stardom see the balance in their relationship with their appreciative public and acknowledge that the public is a partner in their success. In fact, the only exception I ever met was Tommy Hunter who once told me, after a prolonged conversational exchange with fans, that lots of people play guitar as well as he does, but that he knows who has made him what he is, that his most successful talent is keeping the partnership between himself and his fans uppermost in his mind.

I hope, in telling Anne's story, we understand her gift to us a little more and that we understand *her* a little more. And, in a way, because audience and performer are perpetually conducting a relationship, perhaps we even can understand ourselves a little more. Because Anne Murray continues to touch us, with her warmth, her talent, and her drive. Yes, she is over fifty years old. And she is perhaps Canada's only legitimate popular music super-star, along with Bryan Adams, of course. How that came about is not only *her* story but explains the mysterious nature of how she has been able to touch us for so long.

Telling one perhaps tells a little of the other.

CHAPTER ONE

Please Don't Sell Nova Scotia

It may have something to do with with saying 'By God we are going to show those so and so's.' Because we always had the feeling, or I always had the feeling . . . that people were laughing at us. — Anne Murray

Springhill, Nova Scotia, succumbing to the harshness of a mid-1990s early December, seems tired and even morose late on a Monday afternoon. Still, Christmas decorations abound and both pedestrian and vehicular traffic busily negotiate the municipality's small downtown area which seems laid out in a disorderly way, compared to some Canadian downtown cores. Commercial locations are interrupted on a regular basis by homes until the town conveys a sprawl which belies its population of approximately 5,000 people.

Springhill is a mixture of old and new, of refurbished and left-to-its-own designs. Everyone, the town populace, seems to know everyone else; there are hand waves of greeting or those curt, single nods, a nearly imperceptible jerk of the head which are so much a part of the society of small Canadian municipalities. Snow is piled at the sides of the street, whiter than you'd expect, the result of a half-hearted snowstorm just a couple of days earlier. Pedestrians, some of them shopping for Christmas, others running less festive errands, struggle up the steep hill in the middle of town or glide downwards, trying to maintain their footing on the ice as they descend. Everyone is bundled against a brisk wind, has shrunk inside a coat collar.

Springhill might just as well be on the other side of the universe from cities like Toronto or Las Vegas or New York. And perhaps it would be, if not for its common bond with those larger centers — Anne Murray. Due to the careless intricacies of fate, the pop superstar who is a Canadian household name, who has performed in most major entertainment world capitals, who has sold millions and millions of records, was born in and belongs to Springhill, Nova Scotia. It is here that she was raised, attended school, and grew up. It is here from which all that Anne Murray has so far become enjoyed its relatively humble beginnings. And it is here to which she sometimes returns when schedule and her own priorities permit.

These days the connection between Springhill and Anne Murray is not only plainly visible but economically affixed. There are signs advertising the Anne Murray Centre along the major highways in Nova Scotia, from Halifax to Truro where one takes the left turn onto The Trans Canada, heading for the New Brunswick border, then more signs on the way to Exit 9 and Springhill.

The Anne Murray Centre stands out, a new building among a cluster of new buildings which contrast with the older and more run-down sections of town. Right beside it is a Tim Horton's dough-nut and coffee shop which officials at the Centre believe would not be in Springhill if not for the existence of the Anne Murray Centre here, and just across Main Street is the Municipal Building which also houses the Springhill police. Kitty corner from that is the rela-tively new branch of the Canadian Imperial Bank of Commerce, and one wonders if this is by arrangement in view of Murray's promo-tional work with the bank, or purely a coincidence. If you ask someone, they just don't know for sure. From the rooms along one side of the Rollways Motel, Springhill's only motel, where, from time to time, Murray houses a music business guest, the Anne Murray Centre virtually fills the window, just beyond a group of ordinary residences which fill the space in between with palpable incongruity. Just up the street is a Chinese restaurant and down Main Street a few yards, a pizza restaurant. Further away, up on the hill, is the Hilltop Family Restaurant which has a picture of Murray on the dining room wall, autographed. But no-one eats out much this time of year. Stay in Springhill long enough this time of year and you'll eat alone a great deal.

The very fact there exists an Anne Murray Centre, a museum dedicated to the singer's achievements, defines the relationship between pop superstar and community. It is the museum, if you will, which formally ties the knot between them. It is here where Springhill pays tribute to Anne Murray and Anne Murray gives back something to Springhill, her home town. It is the building in which Springhill and Anne Murray arrange to promise not to for-get about one another. It is here where the approved story is told, where the historic connection between town daughter and town is reviewed, where the humble beginnings are related and then contrasted with all that has taken place afterwards on the brighter side of the moon.

"This Centre is dedicated to the people of Springhill for their strength, their courage and their resilience," the singer said July 28, 1989 when the Centre was officially opened.

Since that time, the Anne Murray Centre has become an

important component in Springhill's attempt to encourage a tourist economy in the area, a counterpoint to its long and tragic history as a former coal mining town. There's a curious balance here, as if towns can modestly shrug or scratch their heads at both fame and notoriety.

Not surprisingly there's a certain amount of ambivalence about the Anne Murray Centre and Anne Murray herself, about whether the tourists arrive to find out about her or take a tour of the mine and the other museum which is dedicated to Springhill's coal mining history. It's not difficult to run into someone who went to school with her or who had a brother who went to school with her or who was on hand more than a decade and a half ago when she attended the reunion for Springhill Regional High School, when she performed a new release with some Springhill area musicians and then, according to witnesses, spent six days celebrating the event along with everyone else.

Dave Farnell, for instance, a local carpenter who also works at the Rollways Motel and raises all his own food because a man's better off if he doesn't borrow money, *ever*, was a year behind her in high school. He and his wife, Anne, attended the school reunion in 1978 where she performed with "some of the local fellows."

"I remember her walking down from the hill on the way to high school," remembers Dave. "We all knew she took music lessons but then a lot of kids did. Then she was on that show in Halifax (*Singalong Jubilee*) and then the record came out." He also remembers an autograph session when she was in Springhill on another occasion — "there was a Stedman's then" — autographing her first record. As Dave tells it, she remarked that her name was Anne and she had a brother named Dave, all of which coordinated quite well with Dave and his wife Anne.

He knows, of course, that Murray's mother still lives in Springhill, in the same house where Anne was raised. "I haven't seen her mother in a while but she still lives here." He considers that a moment and adds, "She's a good looking woman for her age." Then it's back to Anne. "We don't see Anne much, she likes to keep out of the public eye. She has a cottage about 30 miles away, near the golf course. Her management sometimes stays at the motel and she picks them up."

Somewhat sheepishly, he makes one confession. "I haven't been to the Anne Murray Centre yet. But I hear it's good."

A local restaurant cook also went to school with the singer. But she's not going to swallow that tourists come to Springhill to visit the Anne Murray Centre. She thinks they journey here to see the mine.

"Anne's not as friendly as she used to be," she adds.

Officially, the Anne Murray Centre was incorporated as a non-profit organization under the Nova Scotia Societies Act and is operated by a Board of Directors representing the Province, the Town and Balmur Ltd., Anne Murray's management company. "Its aim is to provide for public enjoyment a display of artifacts and memorabilia depicting the musical career of Springhill's most famous daughter." Built at a cost of slightly more than $1.5 million, shared on an equal basis by the federal and provincial governments, the Town of Springhill donated the land on which the Centre stands, as well as providing support services throughout the development and construction phases. Balmur has assisted with gathering and coordinating materials for the displays and exhibits. The Canadian Broadcasting Corporation provided support to Balmur and the Board of Directors by assisting with the promotion and editing of the video displays. The building contains approximately 4,000 square feet of floor space on two levels, including 1,700 square feet of exhibition space, a gift shop, and administrative and service areas.

The Centre has already won a national award as an elite Special Project and surpassed projections for its first season's attendance. In fact, it logged more than 25,000 visitors in its first half-season of operation, many of them from Europe, Australia, and South America, as well as from faraway points in North America.

And during the summer of 1990, Anne made an unannounced visit to the Centre to mark the Centre's one-year anniversary. Delighted fans, including a motor coach tour from New York, crowded around to get autographs and pictures with her.

Indeed, the Centre is quite an accomplishment for Springhill and, according to the August 2, 1989 edition of the Springhill and Parrsboro *Record*, the official opening on July 28 drew thousands to downtown Springhill. "When she addressed the screaming, cheering crowd, Murray said that little did she know when her father made her listen to the great voices of the times, or when her mother sent her off to Tatamagouche for singing lessons, or when she travelled to Moncton to perform on CKCW-TV, or played in places like the Colonial Inn in Amherst, or during the first Singalong Jubilee performances, what the future would hold," Kelly Beaton wrote on behalf of the newspaper.

" 'Little did I know that I would be here today standing in front of this building, the tangible realization of twenty years in the entertainment business,' she (Anne Murray) said."

Recounting how Leonard Rambeau had suggested he keep an outfit in which she had appeared in the Rose Bowl Parade in 1972 because someday it might be on display, she confessed to the crowd jamming the area near the Centre that she thought he was crazy.

" 'Nineteen years later, behind me in the Centre, that dress is on display. If you look really closely, you can see that one of the hems was held up by masking tape, which is the way I used to do my sew jobs back in those days,' she joked."

Among the assembled dignitaries was then Nova Scotia Premier John Buchanan, who described Anne as a "world super-star, you are Nova Scotia's superstar, and you are our number one ambassador to the world." According to the local newspaper's report, the crowd was inspired by the reading of congratulatory telegrams. "Congratulatory telegrams from Gov. General Jeanne Sauve, Prime Minister Brian Mulroney, CBC president Pierre Juneau, Bryan Adams, Johnny Cash, Rodney Dangerfield, Corey Hart, Monty Hall, Elizabeth Manley, Randy Travis, Burt Reynolds, Mike Douglas, Dolly Parton, Dusty Springfield, Kenny Rogers and Dionne Warwick were received and read. The crowd reacted wildly to the familiar names."

All in all it was very much an enthusiastic small town scene, the kind one would expect under these circumstances when a native daughter rises to world fame and it can at last be publicly celebrated.

But where Springhill, as a typical Canadian small town, can't help being Springhill, New York can't help being New York and, alas,

Toronto can't help being Toronto. Toronto doesn't always take much to homespun, doesn't seem to understand it, unless of course it's in Toronto and, even then, one borough at a time. And perhaps it's difficult for someone like Anne Murray to straddle the demands of both worlds, the glitter of the world's urban capitols, on the one hand, and the admittedly important connection she feels to the small town where she grew up, on the other. It would appear that what ends up apparently belonging to Toronto is not to be shared legitimately by Springhill.

A brief article by Eve Drobot for the November 1989 issue of *Saturday Night* took a somewhat smarmy approach to the spirit of celebration in Springhill, Nova Scotia, created by the opening of the Anne Murray Centre. "The canonization of St. Anne of Springhill took place under threatening thunderheads in late summer, a bleak day in a bleak little town," the article said. "Right there on Main Street, across from the new bank building and the very old Salvation Army Thrift Shop, stood the spanking new shrine to the woman who had transcended all the local tragedies. Whenever Springhill had made the news before, it was because its men were dying in collapsing coal-mine shafts or its buildings were burning to the ground. And now look — the news was good. Camera crews perched precariously on scaffolding so they could spread the word that *she* had come. Five thousand people, a tad more than the town's current population of 4,800, gathered under the ominous clouds, enduring a never-ending loop of her greatest hits and who knows what other hardships, waiting, waiting, for the triumphal procession."

Asserting that "four years ago, it seems that only divine intervention could right Springhill's seriously derailed economy," Drobot reported that tourism-industry researchers happily predicted 60 to 90 thousand visitors a year. "For centuries," wrote Drobot, "the faithful journeyed to Lourdes, Canterbury, Santiago de Compostela. But that was when we had saints. Today we have singers. The faithful have never lost the urge to flock. Witness the drawing power of Nashville's Grand Ol' Opry, Elvis' Graceland, even Dolly Parton's Dollywood. Now, with any luck, they'll make the pilgrimage to Springhill, Nova Scotia. To be filled with wonder at the exemplary celebrity of a simple doctor's daughter, touched by the angels with a voice of honey, our very own, our pure-piped barefoot girl, Anne Murray."

Drobot's report concluded, "The star's gee-whizzy attitude kept the proceedings down-to-earth. She was not above blaspheming, when the wind hampered her efforts to unveil the dedicatory plaque. 'How the *hell* does this work?' St. Anne implored the heavens. Then in a flash and a fleet of limousines, she and her acolytes were gone. The doors of the reliquary were finally thrown open to the public. Its first visitors were appropriately awe-struck — not least a European gentleman who was delighted to discover that Anne Murray was not dead."

But the Anne Murray Centre is impressive. In it's completeness, in its variety, in the way it brings the singer's world of glamor and fame and riches back to Springhill and insinuates Springhill back into hers.

It comes as no surprise to a visitor familiar with the Murray family and their connection to Springhill that the first major component in the exhibition tribute to Anne Murray's accomplishments is a lighted family tree, tracing more than three hundred years of Murray family history. According to Shelagh Rayworth, executive director of the Anne Murray Centre, the family history was compiled by Murray's brother Bruce, the other noteworthy musician in the family. It traces both sides of the family back to its early 17th-century beginnings in Canada and is an appropriate beginning to this portion of the display focusing on Murray and her family. This is especially true since Murray's mother, Marion, honorary chair of the Anne Murray Centre by the way, and her brother, Stuart, who continues to work at the Springhill correctional institution, still live in Springhill, perhaps a visible reminder that the Murrays remain connected to their roots regardless of the heights of stardom one of them has attained. The Murray home, where Mrs. Murray still resides, sits high on a steep hill which is an integral part of the Springhill geography — people living on the hill are called "hillies" for purposes of reunions and municipal delineation — at 131 Main Street.

Bruce, once part of Anne's musical back up, a recorder of record albums himself, Rayworth will tell you, has decided the constant travel of the music business is not for him. Stuart, too, is musical and performs with local amateur groups from time to time. In fact, the entire family is known to have been musical.

Regardless of what one might think about the complexities in the relationship between a small Canadian town and the musical superstar to which it claims some possession, a tour through the Anne Murray Centre drives the connection home from the very beginning and, even while it begins to focus more and more on Murray's achievements at the international level, sustains that connection throughout. Amid all the glitter, amid the seemingly endless array of awards, video sequences, tributes, gold and platinum records, there is still a homespun feel to the journey through nearly 30 years of musical history. Even an invitation from President Ronald and Mrs. Reagan to Anne and husband Bill Langstroth for dinner, displayed within a collection of other similar memorabilia, seems not a study in contrast between Anne Murray and the town which exists outside, but some kind of *equalizer*, a perspective builder. Rather than demonstrating that a larger, glitzier world exists far from the contrast of Springhill's municipal boundaries, it seems to shrink that contrast, not quite implying that superstardom of one kind or another can happen to just about anyone, but emphasizing that even superstars began their lives as simply *someone*.

Perhaps this sensation of cohesion between the big time and humble beginnings is just a hangover based on the chronological way in which the Anne Murray Centre is laid out. It begins with displays reflecting Anne's childhood in Springhill, everything from wardrobe items through sports paraphernalia to documentation such as report cards and records of vaccinations, photos of Anne as an infant with her family and then childhood, high school, and the mundane progress of growing up. And before we have really embarked on the cataloging of the musical career which has spanned decades, we come face to face with displays about Springhill's coal mining history, a history marked by tragedy, courage, and hardship.

Still, the feeling of unity between Anne Murray and Springhill persists as one explores the early video footage, the early photographs, and the first recording achievements of a long and triumphant career. The bond weakens not at all as the exhibition focuses on her virtually unparalleled success as an international

singer, clings to one's perception even when one reaches the updated exhibits based on her most recent career activities and successes. Even by the time one has reached the end of a seemingly
endless series of tributes and accomplishments, one has the sense
that at least some of Anne Murray's success is *based on* the fact she
originates in Springhill rather than *in spite of* it.

And if this complementary ingredient in success is not directly related to Springhill itself, perhaps its related to the broader
region Canadians call, some in a dismissive way, The Maritimes.
Because this region of Canada, more than any other, has enjoyed
its share of musical success stories. If one believes that drive,
business acumen, development of raw talent, and overcoming
obstacles, even in a large world forum, is the route to success,
then one has to acknowledge that Canada's Maritimes is somehow an ideal place in which to learn and hone those traits.

Perhaps this is what lies at the heart of the ambivalent but per-
sistent connection between Anne Murray and the town where she
was born. Would she have achieved such levels of musical stardom if she had not been born in Springhill, Nova Scotia? Probably.
But had she originated somewhere else, say in a more urban location
in some other region of Canada, would there have been an Anne
Murray Centre to demonstrate the relationship between her point of
origin and her point of international arrival? Probably not.

It's the curious awareness that Maritimers have of a deprecating
opinion of them by points west of there. Even Murray, asked earlier in her career if there is something about the Maritimes that
could be responsible for all the fun she had on *Singalong Jubilee*,
took the opportunity in a promotional interview to explore much
more than that, what might be at the root of musical Maritimers'
drive.

"I don't know. I really can't say. I know the fun was always
there, but creativity, I don't know. It may have something to do
with saying 'By God we are going to show those so and so's.'
Because we always had the feeling, or I always had the feeling,
while on *Singalong* that we were being dumped on by the rest of
the country because people would laugh. They would come down
and watch the show and say 'Oh boy'. But there was some appeal
there. It is like the Don Messer show. You can't dump on that.

People loved it. It's fine. It may not be your cup of tea or my cup of tea, but it is still a good show, and it was well done. And *Singalong*, as I say, we had that feeling about it that people were laughing at us but Maritimers are known for their inferiority complex anyway. I've been through it twice. I had to move from there to here and I didn't move until I knew that they didn't feel that way about me."

One of the video segments in the Anne Murray Centre shows a conversation between Murray and Glen Campbell in which they talk about the relative sizes of their respective communities of origin. Campbell's hometown was under one hundred, he says, and he seems legitimately impressed that Anne Murray's Springhill is much larger. The video clip, from an early period in her career, seems to indicate that Murray was prepared to talk about her community with apparent affection. But then that's why the clip is on display. To demonstrate to the buying public that you can take the star away from Springhill but Springhill can bring her back.

As the December Nova Scotian darkness falls, there is probably not a single tourist in the town at this moment. Yet the lights burn brightly in the museum which Anne Murray's talents built. The gift shop is open for local Christmas shoppers, keeping longer hours so visitors can purchase Christmas presents. As amazing as it seems, as *un*amazing as it seems, the story does indeed begin here, both creatively and psychologically, in Springhill, Nova Scotia. Springhill, perhaps typical in many ways of the Maritimes, knows it and, no matter what is forgotten in the passage of time, Anne Murray knows it too.

C anada is a country of regions, perhaps more so than any other nation in the world. It is the way Canada shrinks itself into a manageable size, at least from the perspective of its residents. It is also the means, for more than half a year, by which its harsh climate is moderated, so that Canadians can focus on a smaller environment within a much larger, much more unrelenting country. This regionalism is the way Canadians define their roots, their sense of home, their influences, the memories which continually shape their present, no matter where in the world their present happens to take them. People in Canada are less Canadians than they are western Canadians, Quebecois, from Ontario or, of course, Maritimers. The characteristics they show, which drive them, which make them who they are, are less the characteristics of a Canadian than they are of an emigrée from a specific Canadian region.

No region in Canada can be proven to be a special fertile ground for the development of artistic or musical talent. Except that the Maritimes, more sparsely populated, as climactically harsh as any in Canada, perhaps the most economically depressed in the country, produces musical stars in direct disproportion to its population. And it can be stated fairly as well that it produces them against overwhelming odds. Although such a conclusion will always be arguable, musical artists from Canada's Maritimes are more independent, driven, and dedicated to their success, pound for pound, than those who hail from elsewhere in this country.

It's not just that a musical heritage has existed in the Maritimes for hundreds of years, not just that enduring there finds its fibers in the creation or performance of music or the enjoyment of it as an audience, but that the Maritimes is an area of the country, generally speaking, more economically challenged than the rest of Canada. Pleasures are simple and festive, snatched like bits of punctuation from long sentences of harsh weather, hard work, and even human tragedy. Those in the Maritimes who wish to make a name for themselves in the world of music may have a rich heritage of music on which to draw but they also have much to overcome.

Which, when you get down to it, is how a talented young woman can rise from a humble municipality like Springhill, Nova Scotia, to become one of the most popular pop singers in the world. The drive to succeed is as Maritime as the Atlantic Ocean, the will to excellence as deeply entrenched as Eastern Canada's rich history. This drive and will and endurance have been apparent in a wide variety of Maritime musical artists. Anne Murray was not the first and it is doubtful she will be the last.

The musical names of the Maritimes strike instant chords with most Canadians and some of them are familiar elsewhere in the world. For nearly 60 years, these musical talents have performed a mix of folk, country, and popular music which is as much a part of the Maritime way of life as eating or sleeping. And those who rose to fame have done so, on occasion, against overwhelming odds. They have staked their claim to music immortality by rising out of harsh, even unhappy circumstances.

Country performer Hank Snow, born in Liverpool, Nova Scotia, in 1914, overcame childhood abuse, a cruel family split up originating with the divorce of his parents, and, in reality, lived much of his childhood as an orphan. He struggled on to musical greatness along with peer Wilf Carter who was born in Port Hilford, Nova Scotia, 10 years earlier. Stompin' Tom Connors was born to a single mother and placed in an orphanage in Saint John, New Brunswick, where, like Hank Snow, he was abused. Eventually calling Prince Edward Island home, he was driven to become a popular and highly successful Canadian artist with his own distinctive brand of music. Rita MacNeil, from Cape Breton in Nova Scotia, overcame arduous circumstances as well to persist with her music until she too achieved stardom.

Other Maritimers have become Canadian household names — New Brunswick native Don Messer, Cape Breton Celtic patriot John Allan Cameron, a long-time friend of Anne Murray, and Bridgewater, Nova Scotia, artist Carroll Baker who has performed with her. And songwriter Gene MacLellan, author of Anne Murray's first smash hit, *Snowbird*, although born in Quebec, called Prince Edward Island home and was, most of all, a Maritimer as an artist.

In Anne Murray's case, home life was not abusive, nor was it economically deprived. Yet, as a native of Springhill, she was brought up in a municipality which seems frankly unsuited to the making of a pop superstar. It was a community which economically struggled, the site of several infamous coal-mining tragedies, a community like so many others in the Maritimes, used to having to overcome the harshness of the elements and difficult economic times.

Whether or not one believes in predestination, when Morna Anne Murray was born at All Saints' Hospital in Springhill on June 20, 1945, her first breaths, whether they would ultimately be musical or not, were taken in an environment rich in musical tradition. And by the time she decided to make music her career, it is likely the Maritime tradition of hard work, overcoming the odds and embracing a fierce independence to succeed on one's own terms were already part of the driving force which would make her a superstar.

Springhill, Nova Scotia is well aware of the two components of its duality with respect to fame. In a sense, its two museums are dedicated to both. While the one finds its focus in a bygone era of harsh circumstance and tragedy, the other celebrates achievement while telling the story of its most famous native. In the sense that all municipalities have a personality, Springhill owns a more provocative version of the same duality which most small, struggling communities demonstrate. On the one hand, it wants to be quaint, on the other, forward looking. On the one hand, it wants to make the most of its history, on the other, it wants somehow to escape its past, move ahead into a more forgiving future. In Springhill's case, it wants to leave behind the notoriety of its ignominious coal mining disasters, or at least lock it into history as an attraction in a burgeoning tourist trade which finds a more positive focus in Anne Murray.

By way of introduction, Springhill Nova Scotia has had much to say about itself over the years. For the record, the Springhill Area Industrial Commission in the latter half of the 1980s described Springhill as "a friendly, hilltop community of four thousand six hundred and sixty-eight population . . . centrally located in Cumberland County, in the northern portion of Nova Scotia, approximately 20 miles from the New Brunswick border." Its location in the Atlantic Provinces was described as "strategic" which made it "an ideal distributing or manufacturing center." According to the industrial commission, its "existing, successful industries have found transportation very adequate. Container ports are available at Halifax (120 miles), St. John (130 miles), and smaller ports at Parrsboro and Pugwash (about 28 miles)." Finally, Springhill offers "the facilities of a 52-acre Industrial Park with land available for expansion."

The Anne Murray Centre, of course, headlined some of the additional amenities, suggesting it would lead to greater tourism development. The other amenities included construction of a $3 million armoury and a pilot project to re-use geo-thermal energy from the warm water in the abandoned mine slopes for "great savings in heating and cooling to larger industry in our park."

There was information about the one Roman Catholic Church and the six Protestant churches, four elementary schools, the Junior-Senior High School Complex and Cumberland Regional Vocational School offering courses in the trades and technical fields. "For girls," notes a promotional brochure, "a hairdressing school and business-commercial course is available."

Notwithstanding the fact Springhill is "close to the Northumberland Strait which offers the warmest salt water of Nova Scotia for swimming and boating . . . trout and salmon fishing are a favourite pastime," Springhill was, in the mid-1980s, much like many Canadian towns of its size with hunting, fishing, skiing, and snowmobiling areas in abundance, a modern stadium for hockey and figure skating, a curling club, a nine-hole golf course, service clubs such as the Rotary and Lions Clubs, the Royal Canadian Legion Branch No. 17, tennis, badminton, and basketball courts, a Chamber of Commerce, a library branch, a pipe band, various church organizations and choirs for men and women, plus the various levels of the Scouting program, fraternal organizations, night school courses, dart and cribbage leagues, programs for senior citizens, a bowling alley, militia and cadets, a ten-lane bowling alley, a pony club and even the Cumberland Firearms Club. It was reported there are annual festivals in Springhill each year as well, events such as Chilli Willi Carnival the last week in February, Old Home Week the last week in July, the Cumberland Craft Festival at the end of September, and the Santa Claus Parade in early December.

The tradition in Springhill is Loyalist. It was first settled in 1790 by three Loyalist veterans who arrived from the United Empire Loyalist Tantramar Colony at Sackville. As a settlement, it grew up near the highest land in Cumberland County, a rounded hilltop 652 feet above sea level. It was called Spring Hill initially because of a large number of springs on the hillside. Early settlers dug coal in the area for their own use, but by 1849 the General Mining Association of London, England, obtained a mining grant of 160 acres. Although this grant was later added to, it did not cover the rich seams of coal. In 1858 mineral rights in Nova Scotia were transferred from Great Britain to the province and other parties secured rights to the area. With the formation of the Springhill Mining Company in 1870, impetus was given to mining on a large scale, a rail line was built to Parrsboro, and the mines were formally opened in 1873. Growing rapidly from five homes in 1871, Springhill, Nova Scotia was incorporated in 1889. Coal mining was the major industry in Springhill, under the ownership of the Cumberland Railway and Coal Company from 1884 until 1911 and then by the Dominion Steel and Coal Corporation. Mine disasters in 1956 and 1958, the second and third such disasters in Springhill's history, brought to an end large scale coal mining at Springhill.

It's a municipality which faces its woes. Not only does it admit to the economic hardship of two major fires on Main Street, one in 1957 and the other in 1975, but the mining disasters are faced with historic pride. The Springhill Miners Museum, in a brochure, asks people to "Visit the friendly Town of Springhill where coal mining has been a way of life and cause of heartache for more than one hundred and forty years." Visitors to Springhill can take in a variety of memorials created in memory of the victims who lost their lives in the major mining disasters. The first was unveiled on September 11, 1894 by Lord and Lady Aberdeen and Sir John Thompson, then Prime Minister of Canada, a memorial in memory of the 125 "men and boys" who lost their lives in the February 21, 1891 explosion. Other memorials were added following the disasters of 1956 and 1958, the former taking 39 lives and the latter taking 75. The second disaster occurred November 1 at 5:07 p.m. with an explosion and a fire which tore through No. 4 Colliery. "Draegermen" and "bare faced miners" rescued 88 men but 39 died. The mine never reopened. The third disaster, in 1958, occurred at 80e years.

This then is the tragic history behind Springhill, Nova Scotia, and a casual portrait of its rather typical small town charm and style. Yet Springhill has courage and drive and, in the face of tragedy, it has an optimism. If, at first, it seems an unlikely beginning for a woman who was to achieve world musical acclaim, one can correlate a municipality's will to prevail with a performer's will to succeed, and Murray herself seems to accept Springhill's importance in her life. Regardless of where she performs in the world, Springhill is mentioned affectionately in on-stage banter and in interviews. Even now, her summer is spent ritually in Nova Scotia, and if the Maritimes has a special magic which creates the kind of wonderful music an entire world can appreciate, well, like so many other musical Maritimers, Murray keeps coming back to renew the solace in her roots.

For Springhill itself, the Anne Murray Centre is a pivotal focus of its tragic history and hopes for the future. As the Centre wishes to point out, "The Anne Murray Centre also contains a special exhibit, featuring Springhill, the brave little town that has raised not only one of North America's most endearing entertainers, but also singing heros of another kind, who performed for their very lives, deep within collapsed coal mine shafts."

At the time, the Anne Murray Centre opened, Springhill was described as "a hardscrabble town, the kind of place where most of the action takes place on the main street, and Saturday night at the Legion is about as wild as the social life gets." The largest local employer, it was reported, was the Springhill Institution, a correctional facility.

When the Anne Murray Centre was officially opened in 1989 as part of Springhill's Centennial celebrations, it was touted as a key tourism initiative and factor in a hoped for economic turnaround for the town. Said Mayor Bill Howard to writer Marilee Little in *The Atlantic Advocate*, "The Anne Murray Centre is going to entice tourists off the Trans Canada (highway) and into Springhill. The flow-through traffic is going to create many opportunities for the private sector. We hope eventually to have additional tourist attractions and then we'll concentrate on trying to keep the tourists for longer than a day's visit. Right now the town has only one small motel, but already two or three developers are interested in getting a larger motel complex in place. Most people view the Centre's opening as the beginning of a turn-around in the town's economic situation." So far, in fact, the motels have failed to materialize.

At the time, many of the town's population were unemployed and the red-brick and white stucco two-story (3,850 square feet) building designed by Amherst architect David Allen, at a value of one and one-half million dollars, was deemed a potential economic boon "for the tiny town with a troubled past."

"It is a pleasure and a privilege to make any contribution I can to a community that has played such an important part in my life," Anne told Little. "My father did it in a more private yet very significant way. I hope I can come close," she added, referring to her father's work as a doctor in Springhill.

The Canadian tradition of self-effacement aside, there can be little doubt that Springhill feels it was destiny that Anne Murray should rise to the giddy heights of superstardom. And whether or not the crowds flock to the Anne Murray Centre in numbers which right the economic wrongs of the town where it is home, it's a matter of balance. Why shouldn't the efforts of a talented and ambitious singer bring fortune to her home town the way it has brought fortune to *her*? When someone else's effort, to make a living and build a life, results in tragedy, surely it is destiny that someone else should offset the tragedy with hope. Not all hard work results in tragedy. Sometimes it leads to success. That's the balance.

This then was home when Murray was born at All Saints' Hospital at 10:40 a.m. in Springhill, Nova Scotia, on June 20, weighing seven pounds, two ounces. It was 1945. There was a riot in Halifax that year when news reached the military that the devastation of World War Two was now over in Europe. These were giddy times for much of the world and a powerful sense of hope characterized the days after the end of a war which had killed more than 30 million people.

In Springhill that year, the same post-war optimism abounded. The town was still a coal-mining center, the next coal mine disaster and the first devastating downtown fire were still 11 and 12 years away, respectively, and, in the wake of six long years of brutal war in Europe and the Pacific, how could things not be much, much better?

All Saints' Hospital is, of course, the only hospital in Springhill, and all of Anne's siblings were born there as well. She is the fourth child of six and the only daughter. The children were raised in the Catholic faith, Anne's mother's, although her father was a Presbyterian. The family tree which is on display at the Anne Murray Centre reveals that her mother, Marion, was the daughter of coal miner Arthur Burke and Mary Beliveau, descended from the

Beliveaus from the Loire Valley in France. Her father, Dr. James Carson Murray, was the son of Dr. Dan Murray and Morna Carson of Tatamagouche, Nova Scotia. The Murrays originated in Rogart, Sutherlandshire, while the Carsons hailed from Dumfries.

Joggins native Marion Margaret Burke was a nurse-in-training while Dr. Murray was a recent medical graduate and, back then, for their respective families a Presbyterian marrying a Roman Catholic was definitely a mixed marriage. As a result, neither one's parents came to the wedding. Raised as Catholics, the children had no negative experiences as a result of the "mixed marriage" except that Anne reported to writer David Livingstone, as a young child, she was once told that eternal salvation was reserved only for Catholics. "How could anyone say that my father wasn't going to heaven? As far as I was concerned, he was the closest thing to God there was," she said, recalling her fear and confusion over the religious assertion which had been presented to her.

Anne was close to her father, a man people described as quietly dedicated, active yet cultured, with a fondness for poetry. Working long hours as a doctor, his recreational pursuits had a tendency to underline a need for privacy and quiet. He ran, hunted, and fished, yet apparently recited Wordsworth. "He used to take us fishing, and when we finished, we'd always go picking Mayflowers. We never caught any fish, but it wasn't until later that I realized that he didn't take us to the best fishing holes. He took us where the Mayflowers were," Anne told Livingstone.

His death in 1980, in early spring, was not only a tremendous personal loss for the Murray family but for the entire community of Springhill where Dr. Murray's dedication was well-known to everyone except perhaps Anne and her brothers. In fact, immediately after his death, when stories were told about his achievements on behalf of the Springhill area citizenry, it was then that Anne learned that her father had made such a significant contribution to his community and, at the same time, had kept these things to himself. In fact, writer Elspeth Cameron, in an article in *Chatelaine*, reported Dr. Murray was "a man revered as a miracle worker by the miners."

An announcement of his death in the April 2, 1980 edition of the Springhill and Parrsboro *Record*, however, is rather subdued. The caption under a front page photograph states: "Dr. J. Carson Murray — a dearly loved, and highly respected citizen of Springhill who served his community faithfully over the years. His sudden passing on Sunday greatly saddened the community as a whole. His funeral will be held at St. John's Roman Catholic Church Wednesday, April 2, at 2 p.m."

On the obituary page of the newspaper, a brief notice covered Dr. Murray's passing: "Dr. James Carson Murray, 72, of Springhill, died Sunday, March 30 in the Halifax Infirmary.

"Born in Tatamagouche, he was a son of the late Dr. Dan and Morna (Carson) Murray.

"He was educated in Tatamagouche, Pictou Academy and Dalhousie University Medical School, graduating in 1932. He did post-graduate work in surgery at Camp Hill Hospital and St. Luke's Hospital, Cleveland, Ohio. He practiced for 45 years in Springhill and was honoured by the town in 1977. He was honoured recently by the Canadian Medical Association.

"He is survived by his wife, the former Marion Burke; a daughter, Anne (Mrs. William Langstroth), Toronto; five sons, Dr. David, St. John's; Daniel, Dartmouth; Dr. Harold, New Glasgow; Stewart, Springhill, and Bruce, Toronto; two sisters, Ethel (Mrs. Bert Livingstone), Earnscliffe, P.E.I., and Betty, Tatamagouche; a brother, Don, Toronto; and 12 grandchildren.

"The funeral service was held Wednesday at 2:00 p.m. in St. John's Roman Catholic Church, Rev. Robert Day officiating, assisted by Rev. James Martell. Commital [sic] was in the Springhill Receiving Vault with burial later in the Spring.

"In lieu of flowers, donations can be made to any charity."

As the town's only surgeon, Dr. Murray made a comfortable living and the Murrays were wealthy enough to have an impressive home, a summer cottage, and a maid, Dena, a woman who came into the Murray household for more than 30 years. Marion Murray, it was reported, was known as Mrs. Murray, the surgeon's wife, as the children were growing up. Prior to that she had taught when she was 16, grades one to ten, and, of course, had worked as a nurse. For the most part, however, she was less a public figure than her much admired husband and her accomplishments, focusing on running the household and raising the children, were more private. Described as a practical person with a great deal of personal strength, Mrs. Murray encouraged her children musically, helped Anne with her only weak subject at school, math, and ran a hospitable and extremely clean and functional household. And, somehow, to boot, she managed to demonstrate what Livingstone calls "a glamorous streak."

Mrs. Murray is reputed to dismiss herself as an unsung factor in Anne's development into what she is today. Even if this point of view is nothing more than self-effacement, it verifies that Anne Murray, almost from early childhood, had her own strong independence and aptitude, regardless of what her mother might want for her or want her to do. Reports Elspeth Cameron: "Marion Murray, Anne's mother, also thought her daughter was special. After three sons, she had hoped for a girl. A devout Roman Catholic, she recalls promising Ste. Anne, the patron saint of housewives and mother of the Virgin Mary, that she would name her child Anne . . . She grew into a 'very active' child, preferring the rough and tumble of boys' games to being dolled up. Eventually, her mother gave up trying. But now she looks back on Anne's life as if willpower and competitiveness had nothing to do with her daughter's success: 'All her life, everything was like a fairy tale. Everything worked for her. It just seemed to snowball.'

"More myth," continues Cameron. "Everything did *not* work for Anne Murray as if she were a saint or a princess. As Anne would put it, to her mother's acute embarrassment, 'I worked my little buns off.'"

As for the tomboyishness, all her siblings were males, and with her father's encouragement in the world of sports — the Anne Murray Centre proudly displays items such as baseball mitts, skates and skis, equipment which belonged to a youngster who admitted to broadcaster Peter Gzowski that she felt uncomfortable wearing dresses — it is not surprising that to hold her own she would develop a drive and competitive edge. Except for her brother Bruce, who also moved into professional music, her brothers moved into careers of their own. Two became doctors like their father, David and Harold, while Daniel became a geologist and Stewart a classification officer at the Springhill medium-security institution.

According to Livingstone, the Murray parents drew boundaries but were not rigid about enforcing them. He reports, however, that Anne's father spanked her once when she was four years old because she wouldn't do what her mother asked her to do. Threatened with "I'll get your father." she said she didn't care. Livingstone says there were no memorable rows later on when she was a teenager and there is no recollection of being told to be in by a certain time.

"In fact," wrote Livingstone, "she laughs to recall the many Friday nights her mother may have wished she were out. While she plastered her bedroom with pin-ups of Tony Dow (he played the Beaver's older brother on the *Leave it to Beaver* television series), Anne felt self-conscious with boys. In her teen years, both sports and singing figured more prominently than dates."

Certainly she was committed to music. The Murrays were a musical clan. Her parents were big on crooners such as Perry Como, while her friends and brothers enjoyed the offerings of the Everly Brothers, Brenda Lee, and Buddy Holly. Anne's favorite was Dusty Springfield. But even with regard to music there would be changes in direction, ambivalent opinions, shifts from style to style and the urgency with which Murray would wish to cross into pop rather than remaining country. In many ways, the various influences would result in an Anne Murray treatment of a wide variety of musical material. Even the crooners she heard by way of her parents in her childhood became material for an album, the recent CROONIN' from EMI.

According to a 1993 *Maclean's* report on the album, "As a little girl growing up in Springhill, N.S., Anne Murray wanted to be 'just like' Doris Day, that clear-voiced paragon of 1950s virtue. When she was a toddler, Murray began singing along to her parents' records by artists like Day, Patti Page and Bing Crosby. And even though as a teenager she was off buying the latest rock releases, the earlier tunes left a lasting impression."

Wrote *Maclean's* Nicholas Jennings: "Speaking to *Maclean's* from a hotel room in Cincinnati, Ohio, midway through a U.S. tour, Murray recalled that recording CROONIN' was a breeze, a 'natural thing to do'. She admitted that the hardest part came from worrying about what singers like Clooney and Day might think of her performance of songs associated with them. Said Murray: 'It was tough because these people were such idols of mine.' But her new album demonstrates that the little girl who sang along with the crooners has gone on to make those tunes her own."

As for country, the genre which initially launched her into stardom, Murray did not care for it as a youngster. "In fact, about the only music Anne Murray didn't like was country music," as she told a writer for *Country Music Beat* in 1975. As a young girl, she was mostly interested in the quality of the voice and intensely disliked most of the country singers she heard on the radio.

Most surprisingly, according to *Billboard* magazine editor Larry Leblanc, in the first heady days of her musical career, Murray had intentions to be done with professional music by the time she was 30 because "she didn't like the music business." Following that, it was said in a number of interviews that she wanted to be a rock singer and only turned to pop because there was more longevity in popular music than for most rock singers. Not only has Murray been prone to changing musical styles but that adjustment in style reflected an uncertainty about whether she wanted to continue with her musical career or not.

It may be that the various changes which have characterized her musical career, the shucking of one image for another, is a direct result of her need to guide her own career — strong management in place of her own business smarts might perhaps have led to a straighter and less rewarding path rather than a career which seems to have reflected changes of mind which in a less public forum would have been taken for granted. Through it all, however, the drive has been there to succeed, and regardless of what she might occasionally claim about her roots not really being a factor, her point of origin in a small mining town in Nova Scotia does compare with other successful Maritimes musical artists who had much to overcome to achieve fame and fortune.

"Anne herself has no easy explanation of what it means to be from the Maritimes," wrote Livingstone. "Searching to summarize the significance of where she grew up, she offers, 'I think it's not taking yourself that seriously. It's a sense of humor and an attitude — no matter what happens, it's not that important.

You're just one little thing in the whole scheme of things.' "

Nice sentiments, perhaps, but somewhat dismissive. In truth, Murray has shown over the years that she takes both herself and her image very seriously. And like it or not, Maritime artists have all shown similar traits, whether raised in a setting of poverty and abuse or whether they came from an economically secure and parentally encouraging domestic environment. It has probably always been true, as Murray said herself, that Maritimers need to work their "buns off."

The Anne Murray Centre on Main Street in Springhill, Nova Scotia, as seen from a room at the town's only motel, the Rollways, with the local branch of the Royal Canadian Legion in the background. Murray was on hand for the sod-turning and the gala opening, and even paid a surprise visit during the first anniversary of the Centre, much to the delight of tourists who happened to be visiting.

The Murray family home at 131 Main Street on the "hill" in Springhill, where Anne grew up and where her mother Marion still resides.

All Saints Hospital is where Anne was born and where her father, Dr James Carson Murray, practiced medicine.

At Springhill High School Anne was a member of a trio called The Freshettes. She attended her school reunion in 1978, performing a version of You Needed Me *before it became her biggest musical hit.*

Members of the Murray family pose for a typical
Canadian family portrait.

CHAPTER TWO

Bidin' My Time

I thought she was singing to me right from the start. The voice went right through me and had me pinned like a specimen to the wall. Voompf! — Bill Langstroth

In Springhill just about everyone you meet has either gone to high school with Anne Murray or has a brother or sister who did. Some of them have photographs to prove it — Anne posing with peers as a cheerleader, something in a yearbook. And the Anne Murray Centre has enough on display from this period in her life to make it seem she went to high school with just about everyone. Unextraordinary stuff that is as normal as normal can be. A pyjamas party photograph, the candid kind where everyone is hamming it up. A picture of Anne and two musical friends known as the Freshettes. That sort of thing.

In high school, she was described as a good student with an athletic bent who, having roughhoused with all those brothers, was a bit of a tomboy who didn't date. There was, of course, those piano and vocal lessons, the bus trips to Tatamagouche on Saturdays for lessons. Here she learned classical music and despite the depth of her alto voice, the training was provided in soprano. Nonetheless, she learned how to breathe, sing harmony, and interpret a variety of musical material. And after one year of musical training, she won top prize for a solo performance of *Primrose* at a local music festival.

Those early days of music seemed as much a moral battleground as an eclecticism of musical styles. On the one hand, she performed *Ave Maria* at her high school graduation and seemed to share her mother's assertion that young people with an interest in music couldn't very well go far astray. "Children who love music," Marion Murray told Elspeth Cameron for *Chatelaine*, "are happy in themselves. They don't get into other things that might be dangerous, things that might lead them astray." On the other hand, her voice had a quality of sensuality which contrasted sharply with the intended strict Catholic upbringing, the upbringing which encouraged Murray to enroll at Mount St. Vincent, a Halifax Catholic women's college. It is now well documented how, during her year at Mount St. Vincent, her rehearsed rendition of *Summertime* disturbed a nun at the college. When the nun complained that Murray's version made her sound Black, Murray was puzzled and hurt. Although she was told to change her approach to the song, she ultimately performed it at the concert in the fashion she wished. Reports Cameron: "I suppose she was a bit of a rebel," her mother admits. "But the audience loved it."

And husband Bill Langstroth later claimed that he too felt a thrilling sensuality in Murray's voice when he first heard it during auditions for *Singalong Jubilee*. "I thought she was singing to me right from the start. The voice went right through me and had me pinned like a specimen to the wall. Voompf!" he told Cameron.

But that was a little later. In the meantime, during her summer vacation after the one year at Mount St. Vincent, she took a job at the Keltic Lodge in Ingonish, Nova Scotia. There, when she wasn't making her living as a maid, she formed a group with a couple of other employees and, on occasion, they entertained guests at the lodge, performing material by the likes of the Kingston Trio and Peter, Paul and Mary.

The following autumn she began studies at the University of New Brunswick in Fredericton where, three years later, she would graduate with a degree in physical education. It was during this period at college that she made her first tentative move in the direction of a musical career. The year was 1964 and the program was CBC-TV's summer show *Singalong Jubilee*.

One of the best definitions of just what Maritime music is all about in Nova Scotia originates from the pen of Bill Howell in a 1972 article on Anne Murray for *Maclean's*. "Music in Halifax is what happened when the end-of-the-line underground railroad blues met a North Atlantic storm of self-protective irony. The northend black music fed on the blacker sea shanties on ships with grass, hash and heroin hidden in their fire hoses and the popular music of the world on their public address systems," he said then.

A colorful way of putting it, perhaps, but it still rings true. When Murray auditioned in 1964, she was coming in on the late stages of a powerful musical environment defined by the tradition of Hank Snow, blues, country and Celtic music, a strange accumulation of musical styles embroidered by popular appeal and a practical approach to performing it. And although it virtually goes without saying that the resulting musical collision was popular in the Maritimes, it was often just as popular elsewhere in Canada. Witness the emergence of Don Messer and his Islanders in

1956 who began a startling rise to popularity at CBHT-TV in Charlottetown. Soon the weekly show, *Don Messer's Jubilee*, would rise to such national popularity that it would be second only to *Hockey Night in Canada* as the prime television diversion for Canadian viewers. Its producer was a young Haligonian named Bill Langstroth, described by some as a pioneer in Canadian television.

Langstroth was called upon in 1960 to produce a summer replacement for his Don Messer show, and American folksinger Pete Seeger taped the pilot for the replacement called *Folksong Jubilee*. Nonetheless, Seeger's notoriety with the American government and his affiliation with the civil rights movement in the United States were enough to have the CBC and the sponsor of the program pull the plug. As Howell comments, "They weren't about to be brave enough to broadcast the voice of the North American subconscious yet, so the show was canned, Seeger's career held up, and Langstroth rushed himself into the Seeger roll with another new pilot to salvage the summer and make sure everybody's cakes were baked right. Thus, from Seeger, came the first musical rule for the city: do the best you can with what you've got on hand." Howell also pointed out in 1972 that the Seeger pilot is missing from CBC Program Archives.

The resulting program was *Singalong Jubilee* which would bring together a wide variety of musical talent including Langstroth himself, Catherine McKinnon, Jim Bennet, The Don Burke Four, and blind flat-top guitarist Fred McKenna, whom Anne Murray says ended her lack of appreciation for country music. Ultimately, the program signed with Canadian-owned Arc records for a series of albums through Bill Gilliland, a Torontonian but living in Halifax. Although Arc believed in Maritime talent, it also was practical enough to know that the talent, for the interim, would have to be offered at discount record prices in music stores throughout the land. Nonetheless McKinnon went on to sell 200,000 copies of her first album which was produced by Brian Ahern who would ultimately take Anne Murray to Capitol Records and produce the first batch of her many recording enterprises.

Although Murray showed up to audition in 1964 for *Singalong Jubilee*, she did not obtain employment on the series. One of dozens to audition, she was narrowed down to one of two but, ultimately, she was not needed. They were up to their necks in altos. Nonetheless, Langstroth advised her to stay in touch because the situation could change. True to his word, the two were in contact two years later, although Murray had to be encouraged to audition yet again.

According to some music industry promotional material issued in the mid-1970s, Langstroth said, "We had all the altos we could handle. You just know when you run into a goodie like her. I thought she was sensational. She was even better two years later when I called her back for another audition. She told me to stuff it. She said 'You'd better have a job for me.' She knew she could sing better than the kids on the show. She could. She was great."

A similar version appears in the *Encyclopedia of Folk, Country & Western Music* in 1984, by Irwin Stambler and Grelan Landon. "But she stuck in the mind of both Langstroth and his associate Brian Ahern. Two years later Langstroth wired and cabled the university trying to find her. When he did, she wasn't interested; she had decided she would take her B.A. and teach physical education in high school. 'She gave me a lot of lip,' Langstroth said. 'I told her she should try again. She said, No way, I'm not coming to your stupid auditions. But I kept talking and she showed up and we hired her.' " She was on the show for four seasons. Ultimately, she did teach a year of high school on Prince Edward Island, continuing with *Singalong Jubilee* in the summers and getting time off from school late on Fridays to perform local gigs.

Howell's *Maclean's* article offers a more tepid version of Murray's initial impact on the show, however. "Anne Murray showed up for chorus work on *Singalong* in the summer of 1966 and nobody thought she was great. But her warm, pure, lyrical alto was a welcomed part of a great new influx of talent to the show, most of it around twenty-one years old then, all of it Maritime: John Allen Cameron, an Oblate disciple from Mabou, Cape Breton, who sang his music better than anyone else in that wild Scottish Irish 12-string world of his; Edith Butler, a superb Acadian folk singer from Paquetville, New Brunswick; Ken Tobias, from Saint John, who would later write *Stay Awhile* for the Bells; and Steve Rhymer from Yarmouth-Dartsmouth-Halifax, who wrote *No One Is To*

Blame for Anne . . . But it was the great blind flattop picker Fred McKenna, who just sat there and grinned and seemed to know what everything was all about, who insured that the doctor's daughter from Springhill and anyone else who heard (and still hears) him would never be the same again."

All the factors and personalities of what would ultimately be the making of a musical superstar were now falling into place.

In the period not long before Murray joined the cast of *Singalong Jubilee*, the CBC was inadvertently acting as a further catalyst to the making of a musical career. Deciding in the mid-1960s to launch a rock 'n' roll program to run every weekday afternoon from 5:30 to 6:00, the CBC came up with *Music Hop*. The premise of the show was to expose top forty records to teenagers with the program originating from different Canadian cities each day, namely from Halifax, Montreal, Toronto, Winnipeg, and Vancouver. Strangely, live music was forbidden in all the cities but Toronto; the other locations were to serve up a menu strictly composed of records.

As Bill Howell in *Maclean's* observes, "Because by then the blues in the largest black settlement in Canada was beginning to get public, with the help of a little Nova Scotia Light and Power, *Music Hop* started out in Halifax in the winter of 1965-66 according to the Toronto Rule Book, but eventually producer Manny Pittson couldn't help himself. His part of the series was called *Frank's Bandstand* after host Frank Cameron, a Halifax disc jockey, but right away it starred Brian Ahern and The Off-beats, who joined Karen Oxley, Patrician-Ann (McKinnon), and great black performers like Davy Wells and the Raindrops to produce the new Halifax Sound . . . But Brian Ahern felt that Maritime talent deserved more than crummy ninety-nine-cent records in the drugstores of the country. Rule Number Two was his: 'Make a five-year plan.' He left for Toronto."

Ironically, Howell and Ahern grew up approximately two blocks from one another, "but we didn't know each other well, we went to different schools." Howell reports that Ahern "used to drive around town on a special bicycle with a transistor radio screwed into its crossbar, wearing a red scarf and a buckskin jacket with Wild Bill Hickock fringe. And once, in our early teens, I met him standing with his guitar in the middle of South Street at dusk in the fog, singing *Your Cheatin' Heart*. He was a weird kid, but fun." Tourists visiting the Anne Murray Centre in Springhill get to meet Ahern in a video clip. Murray explains that he is her record producer. Ahern is stiff, with long hair and a wispy goatee, and has the look of a man who has some private and faintly humorous secret forever on his mind.

But by 1967 he was departing Halifax for Toronto with the ambition of becoming a record producer. As a result, he took a job with Gilliland at Arc Records and Bay studios and began to teach himself to become a record producer. Ultimately, Ahern would call Murray while she was teaching in Summerside and ask her to do an album with him. Even more ultimately he would move to Los Angeles, marry Emmylou Harris, and live out his ambition to conquer his slice of the musical world.

It was Ahern and Langstroth together who began to try to convince Murray that she should devote full time to music. "Ahern in particular was anxious to groom her for recording work," says Stambler and Landon's *Encyclopedia*. "As she told Bobby Allen for an article in *Country Music* (July/August 1979), 'I remember when I was still teaching [at a high school on Prince Edward Island], Brian Ahern sent me special delivery letters telling me to come on up to Toronto where he was learning to be a record producer. I thought he was crazy! In fact, when I did finally get there, I remember going down to the hock shop to get two of his guitars out of hock. That's how badly off he was. That was in the fall of '68.' "

Nonetheless, Ahern was able to persevere and provided Murray with the opportunity to record her first album, WHAT ABOUT ME, on Arc Records. And Murray had finally decided to give up teaching. She resigned her teaching position to become a regular on *Let's Go*, another program shot in Halifax, adding it to her *Singalong Jubilee* work.

Amidst the kind of frenetic humor surrounding the *Singalong Jubilee* days, as they are presented in videos at the Anne Murray Centre, songs belted out while hastily pumping a railroad handcar around the tracks, hotly pursued by a belching locomotive, and other such memories, there is a more sober presence of tragedy. 1995 was the year that Anne Murray endured two personal tragedies, the death of personal manager and close friend Leonard Rambeau, and the suicide of gifted musician and songwriter Gene MacLellan. A video in the museum shows Anne in conversation with MacLellan, his left eye covered by a patch, both of them discussing the possible creative reasons for the success of the major hit he penned, *Snowbird*. And at the entrance to the long series of displays there is the acknowledgement of Leonard Rambeau, described as Murray's manager, mentor, and friend. Rambeau died of cancer just before Easter in 1995. He was only 49 years old, leaving behind his wife, Caron, and their three children. Not long before his death, he had been given the Global Achievement Award at the 1995 Juno Awards by the Canadian Academy of Recording Arts and Sciences. It was only death which could end the long association between Murray and Rambeau. In fact, it is somewhat ironic that this simple but powerful tribute should appear the way it does in the Anne Murray Centre, in view of the fact that in some circles the idea to establish the Centre was initially Rambeau's.

Said *Toronto Star* entertainment columnist Sid Adilman not long before Rambeau's death, "It was Rambeau's idea to establish the Anne Murray Centre at her birthplace of Springhill, N.S. From its start in 1989, the museum has been a popular tourist site." Adilman also quotes the anecdote Murray initially outlined during the Centre's opening ceremonies about her Rose Bowl Parade outfit, the way it was repaired with masking tape, and how the outfit is on display at the Centre.

Described by Canadian *Billboard* editor Larry LeBlanc as one of the most respected people in the Canadian music industry, Leonard Theodore Rambeau originally hailed from Cape Breton. According to a 1973 *RPM* profile, Rambeau's first contact with Murray was on December 16, 1968 when he hired her for a benefit he produced for a youth club in Dartmouth. For that particular performance she received $125. "Then," said Rambeau, "the following year I was approached by the Alumni Association of Saint Mary's University to produce a show for them and she did a concert for $900, which included the musicians. It was the night before the first Capital album, THIS WAY IS MY WAY, was released. At the reception afterwards, Anne came up to me and said that if she decided to stay in the business she'd hire me as a road manager. I thanked her and then ran home to look up the definition of road manager."

According to *RPM*, Rambeau at the time was employed by the federal government as a student placement officer at Saint Mary's. Ahead of him was a career defined by security and the prospect of regulated advancement. But he began to see more of Anne Murray and escorted her to basketball games and shows, noting that he could see where some organizational assistance was needed. "I started to see things that bothered me. Like press releases weren't being sent out to the big Toronto machine. Nobody really knew what was happening — she just went and did things. And the fan mail business wasn't being taken care of. She isn't one to write letters so all that mail was piling up. I invested the grand sum of sixteen dollars to get a post office box to keep the mail away from her apartment."

Then, in December of 1970, after Murray displayed her bare feet to a "posh Toronto audience at the Royal York Hotel," Rambeau left his job with the government for a week to get her through what was a nervous booking. Ultimately, he joined her permanently in Toronto the following April. It has been reported more than once that Murray chose Rambeau over a cluster of prospective other managers "determined to get their claws into her rising star" because she believed he would be honest with her. "But," said Rambeau, "it was a tough decision to make. I had a secure job with the government. Show business? Well . . . it could all end tomorrow. And she had delayed asking me because she knew she couldn't match the security of my job. Nick Sevano was handling her affairs in Los Angeles but up here she was even paying the band herself."

Rambeau picked up the pieces in a style which would demonstrate his future managerial abilities. And Anne Murray would learn the value of employing a manager whom she could trust. As he explained in 1973 to *RPM*, "It's been a relief for both of us, this mutual trust and friendship. We've never had an argument. Each of us knows instinctively that the other will do what has to be done and do it right."

For approximately 25 years, until his death, Leonard Rambeau would remain as the capable organizer behind the scenes of Anne Murray and her company, Balmur, which incorporates letters from her name, Rambeau's name and Brian Ahern's name, as well as Bill Langstroth's moniker. And, according to Sid Adilman, Murray and Rambeau did not have a contract. " 'Never needed one,' he said in a recent interview. 'Maybe that's one of the reasons the relationship has lasted. Neither of us has a piece of paper we can throw at a lawyer. It's just mutual trust and respect.' " (The 1973 *RPM* article, however, does mention that signatures were exchanged, presumably to form Balmur itself. "I arrived at the [Murray] apartment at 6:15 and at 7:00 I was sitting in a meeting with Anne's accountant. The company had already been formed and they were waiting for me to arrive to sign the papers.") Murray is also quoted as saying, "We've never had an argument. He's no desk-pounder."

Rambeau's impact on Balmur would not only focus on his partnership with Anne Murray but permit the company to handle other musical acts as well, from John Allan Cameron and Robbie MacNeill in the early days to Balmur's current projects, Rita MacNeil and Alberta country singer George Fox. Over the years he was known in an often hostile pop music industry as "a class guy whose word is his bond."

After his death, Murray said Rambeau was the guiding light of her career. "I've always said that Leonard was the only indispensable person in my career," she said in a statement. "It is hard to imagine my life or my career without him." And so it was that the man who had rushed home to look up the definition of road manager arrived on the scenes to help steer Anne Murray's career which, thanks to the success of *Snowbird,* was now on a runaway course.

The writer of *Snowbird* died just a few months before Rambeau, a suicide, and Anne Murray ran a full-page sympathy advertisement in *The Record,* one of the recording industries primary trade publications. When Gene MacLellan died in January of 1995, it closed the book on one of Canada's most enigmatic and talented songwriters and musicians. For most, the runaway popularity of the song was unexpected and there are those who maintain that, for MacLellan, success was not necessarily a welcome development. Although it launched the career of Anne Murray, and would sometimes be the butt of rehearsal jokes by Murray and her musicians a number of years later, it seemed an unlikely melody for a smash hit. Richard Flohil's *Canadian Musician* report is an example. "The rehearsal at the L.S. Beatty Secondary School — her management have hired the auditorium for three weeks so she can prepare for the tour — is going well enough for Murray to kid around, especially as she goes through *Snowbird* yet another time, singing every single note deliberately off key, and with every member of the band playing agonizingly out of tune. (Several years ago, this writer watched Murray rehearse the same song with the Toronto Symphony for a Musicians Union benefit concert — as she hit the final note of *Snowbird* a full semitone sharp, every member of the orchestra looked at her with shock and horror, while her band members howled with laughter)."

But, back then, at the beginning of the 1970s decade, the *Singalong Jubilee* connection was continuing to mesh and Bill Langstroth continued to be the catalyst. It was Langstroth who contacted Murray, reported coming across a songwriter named Gene MacLellan, and suggested that she give *Snowbird* a listen as possible recording material. She did and a hit record was born.

Anne appears barefoot in this 1967 publicity photo for Singalong Jubilee.

The Freshettes (Geraldine Hopkins, Anne Murray, Catherine Ross) reunited for a class reunion, complete with Anne's trademark ukelele.

Anne Murray performing on
Singalong Jubilee.

CHAPTER THREE

Fly Away With Me

We went to Capitol and we told them everything we wanted and they gave it to us. We were flabbergasted. They must have known something we didn't.

— Anne Murray

Any examination of modern Maritime music is seriously lacking if it does not include the work of Gene MacLellan, regardless of the impact of his song *Snowbird* on the career of Anne Murray. Although MacLellan is definitely a Maritimes artist, he was born in Val d'Or, Quebec, in 1939, and then later moved to Toronto while still a small child. In fact, he didn't reach the Maritimes until 1964, more or less wandering in that direction, traveling and taking odd jobs from the age of eighteen onwards.

The enigma about Gene MacLellan is the almost grudging way in which he approached musical success. He was reputed to be among the most private musicians in Canada and, after he reached the zenith of his songwriting success in the early 1970s, suddenly virtually vanished from concert stages. Although some critics say *Snowbird* categorically defines his songwriting style, it was after the success of this song that he disappeared from the limelight for a long period of time. Nonetheless, there were other successes such as *Put Your Hand In The Hand* and tunes considered country classics: *Pages of Time, Thorn In My Shoe, Hard As I Try, Bidin' My Time, The Call.*

Music was part of MacLellan's life from an early age. He was already an accomplished acoustic guitarist by the age of ten and he fit into the new Toronto music scene early. The Band's Robbie Robertson was one of those with whom MacLellan performed in a group in the early days. And ultimately he played with Little Caesar and The Consuls, a successful Toronto early 1960s group.

By the time he lived in Prince Edward Island, MacLellan was playing back-up guitar and was building a reputation as a very talented musician. It is reported that he performed with Lena Welsh who would go on to marry Stompin' Tom Connors. Following a car accident which dislocated his shoulder and laid him up for several months, MacLellan took the mishap as an indication that he should settle down and embrace a musical career once and for all. By 1966, he had been invited to play on the Langstroth CBC production *Don Messer's Jubilee* and this further led to prolonged engagements with Hal "Lonepine" Breau, father of the legendary Lenny Breau who would perform in Anne Murray's band, Richard, throughout the early 1970s. It was after his work with Don Messer that MacLellan was offered work as a regular cast member and songwriter on *Singalong Jubilee*. Because MacLellan was adept in virtually every musical genre, the program was able to make good use of his versatility and solo ability.

But even then, there was a provocative air of mystery around Gene MacLellan. Often he would disappear for days without a word and then report that he had returned to Prince Edward Island, the place he claimed lived at the root of his creativity. *Snowbird* was only his second composition, but MacLellan later claimed there was a lot of himself in the song, a reflection of his travels and the things which were important to him. Although Anne Murray, he later said, was his favorite singer at the time, he did not write it with her in mind, which only added to the apparent unexpectedness of the song's phenomenal popularity both in Canada and the United States.

Although Murray also recorded two other MacLellan songs on her second album — the first for Capitol Records — THIS WAY IS MY WAY, namely *Bidin' My Time* and *Hard As I Try*, it was *Snowbird* which, of course, prompted a rash of concert tours and appearances. MacLellan seemed unprepared for this kind of success, for the speed with which things were happening to him. Although he managed guest slots on television programs hosted by Tommy Hunter or Ian Tyson, although he would record three solo albums for Capitol Records — GENE MACLELLAN, STREETCORNER PREACHER, and IF IT'S ALL RIGHT WITH YOU — it was reported that the hectic pace of musical stardom was shattering his nerves and wearing down his health. Soon married, he retreated to his beloved Prince Edward Island and tried to regain some perspective.

Still, when success comes calling it often will not relent. MacLellan was to have no peace from the success of his songwriting talents. In 1971, Ocean recorded MacLellan's gospel tune *Put Your Hand In The Hand* and the song sold nearly three million records. Anne Murray, it would be revealed later, wanted to release the song as a single prior to Ocean, but Capitol Records would turn down the idea, to their own detriment, being content to have the song appear on Murray's 1970 album, HONEY, WHEAT & LAUGHTER.

As Bill Howell observed at the time: "Certainly the most costly management decision in Anne's career so far has been on the part of Capitol Records. *Put Your Hand In The Hand*, another Gene MacLellan song, would have made it on the Top 40 if Capitol had done what everyone here wanted and released it as a single. But they left it on the album, and sly old Bill Gilliland at Arc rushed through a 'throwaway' single with the rock group Ocean, using the same arrangement as Anne's album version but with a steadier rhythm track. Ocean's version sold three million, and there was a major headhunting expedition in Capitol (U.S.) over that."

With the success of this new song, MacLellan more or less faced the fact that he was primarily a songwriter. Intrigued by classical guitar, he took lessons on the wider-necked instrument and began to apply it to his playing and his future compositions. Staying out of the public eye as much as possible, he remarried after his first marriage ended in divorce and moved back to Ontario, settling in Burlington. MacLellan rarely made public appearances, with the exception of CBC Radio's *Ocean Limited* in 1984 and *Swinging on a Star* in 1990.

By the time MacLellan returned to Prince Edward Island with his family, it was reported that he had at last found happiness in his personal life and had resumed his creative work. On a ritual basis he kept in touch with Balmur, perhaps once a year, to advise them if he had a song in which Murray might be interested. Overall, however, after the initial songwriting success which so apparently mystified him, MacLellan was generally a forgotten man in Canadian music until his death in January of 1995.

As such, the cast and the circumstances were virtually complete for the meteoric career of Anne Murray. Overall, the music industry is a small club, hardly more than a small city in population. This shrunken circumstance is even more applicable when one considers the relative size of Canada's Maritimes and the Maritime music industry. No wonder the musical circle was complete: Bill Langstroth, Brian Ahern, Gene MacLellan, *Singalong Jubilee*. And Anne Murray, of course, a woman about to embark on a recording career which would ultimately make her one of the world's reigning pop music stars. And perhaps it would coin the phrase Maritime Mafia, a term Anne Murray would make self-allowance for, explaining that when she used it during a Juno Award ceremony she was not well at the time. Nonetheless, it was a term which would stick. Bill Howell's 1972 *Maclean's* article features it strongly in its subtitle: *Another* Goin' Down The Road *smash hit, starring Anne Murray, the Maritime Mafia and a host of other swell folks.*

WHAT ABOUT ME, Anne Murray's first album in 1968, produced by Ahern and containing liner notes by Langstroth, was cut in Toronto on the Arc label and cost a reported $3,000. It presented a mixed bag of material and reflected that contemporary and folk music were the reigning musical genres of the time. Ironically, although at first Anne Murray would be considered a country artist, there was only one country song on this album, a tune called *There Goes My Everything.* Other offerings included fellow Canadian Joni Mitchell's *Both Sides Now* and the always prerequisite Bob Dylan song for the times, *Last Thing On My Mind.* The album sold moderately well by all reports but launched a Murray-Ahern relationship which would last for ten albums.

Folk and pop were the prime items on Murray's menu at the time when she began to back up the album's release with a tour of Nova Scotia gymnasiums, coffeehouses, and clubs, complete with a back up band. To overstate her informal stage presence, Murray took to performing in bare feet. Photographs also show her playing guitar, although she is listed in Stambler and Landon's *Encyclopedia* as a ukulele player. The barefoot performing, long after she abandoned it, would come back to haunt in such nicknames as Barefoot Annie, the Annie coined by American audiences who saw her image as a down home sweetheart, a girl next door one would have to call Annie.

During this period, another coincidentally brief Maritime connection was about to be made. Skip Beckwith (referred to in early profiles of Murray as "Skipper"), a jazz bass player, heard her perform at Confederation Place in Charlottetown, Prince Edward Island. In the oft mentioned intimacy of the music business, Beckwith was already acquainted with Brian Ahern, reportedly because they shared an interest in jazz and because they both hailed originally from Halifax where they sometimes played together in a fraternity house in which they both were members. Beckwith later recalled, "The quality of her singing was incredible. She was dead in tune and she had this very interesting voice which nobody had ever heard anything about. Really, nobody had ever heard anything like that before."

By the time Beckwith returned to Toronto, Ahern called him and asked him to round up musicians for an Anne Murray recording. Among the musicians to play on the album with Beckwith were Ahern himself on guitar, Amos Garret, Buddy Cage, Mike Burbey, Brian Browne, Pat Riccio Jr., Eric Robertson, Ron Rully, Tommy Graham, and John Pace. Beckwith and Ahern had, by this time, formed a company called Happy Sack Productions.

On the eve of Murray's signing with Capitol Records-EMI of Canada, there were additional, somewhat nationalistic forces in Canada at work which would help Murray and other Canadian artists to receive the radio airplay they had often been denied in the past by an aggressive American music market. For one thing, the CRTC was preparing to mandate a 30 percent Canadian content requirement on Canadian radio stations. Linked to this was a strong sense of Canadian nationalism, partially generated in 1967 by the emotional fervor surrounding Canada's celebration of its first hundred years as a nation. Not only was Canada about to get a regulation-induced serving up of its own homegrown talent, the country was actually in the mood for it.

As for Capitol, part of the British EMI giant, a deal appealed to Anne Murray and Ahern because it would mean exposure to American audiences through its U.S. Capitol arm. Not only would Murray and her partners be pleased to sign on with Capitol in 1970, but Capitol would be pleased to sign them.

Capitol Canada was already embroiled in the tail end of an evolutionary process from being solely a distributorship prior to the turbulently musical 1960s to actually finding, signing, and recording its own talent. By the time Anne Murray and company entered the Capitol offices for discussions, Capitol had evolved from its distributor role to the signing company for Jack London and the Sparrow, later Steppenwolf (now John Kay and Steppenwolf), the Staccatos from Ottawa, later the Five Man Electrical Band, and Edward Bear. The man behind many of the signings was Paul White, who claimed in a publicity article which was part of a promotional package issued early in Murray's career, to have come into the business "through the shipping room window." White, later with Balmur, became Capitol's A&R man virtually by accident but was the man with whom the Murray entourage met in 1970 to come up with the record contract which would result in her first album and the hit single *Snowbird*.

Strangely enough, the promotional material designed to promote Murray features not only an interview with Murray herself, but also behind the scenes articles on Langstroth, Ahern, and White. The result is an apparently conflicting report, on the surface at least, of just who sought out whom in those early days before Murray was signed to Capitol. It was a meeting apparently blessed by an air of serendipity.

The Murray version was elicited by this question in the promotional article: "How did you come to sign with Capitol?"

"We wanted a bigger company, one that was a U.S. subsidiary," replied Murray in the article. "We went around to a couple of them, and they said they would give us three thousand dollars to do it, but they wanted to be in on the production. Even at Arc, Brian (Ahern) had the creative freedom. So we went to Capitol and we told them everything we wanted and they gave it to us. We were just flabbergasted. They must have known something we didn't. Brian had spent so much time convincing me that I was the greatest thing since sliced bread. He kept saying 'Now listen, before we go out to talk to the record companies, you are the most talented broad in the world and I'm the most talented producer in the world and together we are going to do it.' And this is the attitude that we had to approach them with. I said 'O.K. Brian', not believing it for one minute. When we went, I got what I expected from the other record companies, but when we went into Paul White and said 'We want this and we want that', and by that time I was almost convinced, he said 'Fine'. They gave us eighteen thousand dollars to do the album."

Paul White in the same promotional document reported, "I started watching *Singalong Jubilee*, which was a rotten show, and every now and again, out would trot this little blonde without any shoes on. Every time she came out, she was refreshing. I checked her out and found that she was already on another label (Arc). Then one of our salesmen from the east called and said she was trying to get another label. It was hard to track her down; but eventually, one of our salesmen, Alan Clark, found her. We made a date to talk the next week in Toronto.

"A week later, after traipsing through and being dissatisfied with the offers forthcoming from Capitol's competitors, Anne, Brian Ahern and Bill Langstroth entered Paul White's domain. 'It was the easiest afternoon I've ever spent in my life,' says White. 'I don't think they came up with anything we couldn't go along with. I think at the end of the afternoon, without anything being decided on our part, I knew we were going to sign Anne Murray.' "

According to White the contract was signed a week later, providing for two record albums per year, and, within a month, everyone was in the recording studio producing THIS WAY IS MY WAY. White, by the way, wrote the liner notes for the back of the album. "When the album was complete, White proudly played it for Capitol sales staff. A gentleman, who is no longer with Capitol, passed the observation that it would, of course, 'appear on the $1.98 label'. 'That's when I had my biggest fight with any-one over Anne,' says White. 'I said she's a five dollar artist and that's that. I don't think I spoke to him for quite a long time.' "

In the same promotional article, an apparently self-effacing White clears up that *Snowbird* was not the first single recording for Anne. "Although most people persist in believing that *Snowbird* was Anne's first single, or the 'B' side of it anyway, White states that the first single was in fact *Thirsty Boots*, the Eric Anderson tune. Says White, 'At the time, I thought she was going to be another Judy Collins. Brian, Skip and I were in Bay Studios. Brian said, 'Okay, you're the A & R man, you pick the single.' We brought the bloody thing out and we were lucky to sell a thousand copies."

It was the insistence of one of Capitol's American executives that *Snowbird* appear as the "B" side of *Bidin' My Time* in the United States. "Says White, 'A guy named Happy Wilson worked his butt off and went around to every radio station in the coun-try, pushing *Bidin' My Time*. It started showing up in the tip sheets, and then the radio stations began listening to the flip. Then the stations in Canada followed. It went on to become a million-seller."

In view of its impact on Murray and the rewards it brought to her and Capitol Records, as well as a reluctant Gene MacLellan, it is ironic that *Snowbird* backed its way into gold record status. In fact, by today's standards, even with a budget of eighteen thousand dollars, THIS WAY IS MY WAY was a modest venture. According to Skip Beckwith, much of the work was done at an eight-track studio in the north end of Toronto and a good deal of the arranging was improvised from a melody sheet with chord symbols. Add some of Ahern's overdubbing tracks of steel guitar or piano as required and that was it. But the recording of *Snowbird* did have a little extra. Beckwith reports that Ahern thought the string arrangement on the song, provided by Toronto arranger Rick Wilkins, was the proverbial icing on the cake. Although *Singalong Jubilee* was well represented on the album — also included were two other tunes by MacLellan, *Bidin' My Time* and *Hard as I Try*, as well as *No One Is To Blame* by *Jubilee* alumnus Steve Rhymer — *Snowbird* had found that middle ground between country and pop which popularized it with millions who had a taste for one or the other. Characterized by a gentle country beat and by Wilkins' gliding string accompaniment, its lyrics generated a response in people who felt touched by its delicate sense of regret. For many music critics, *Snowbird* is considered the first of what would become known as the crossover hit, palatable to easy listening audiences who didn't like country as well as country audiences who generally didn't like any other musical genre.

The wake which follows the speedboat of success, however, has two ridges, one full of accolades and royalty checks, the other containing the obligations surrounding what to do next. And the surprise factor of such a hit record is inevitable for most music artists the first time around. Few are already prepared for what must follow to maintain the momentum of success. In Murray's case, on the heels of the million-selling momentum of *Snowbird*, what followed was a hectic and arduous several months. On the accolade side, *Snowbird* was rising steadily on Canadian and American charts in June. The following month, Murray was signed to an exclusive two-year radio and television contract with the CBC. And in Los Angeles, the producers of Glen Campbell's television show, *The Glen Campbell Goodtime Hour*, were making inquiries to avail themselves of her services there. When Murray left for L.A. in early September, crowds showed up in Halifax to give her a send-off. Not only were there several appearances on the Glen Campbell television show, but she was presented with her first gold record on the *Merv Griffin Show* in November.

At the same time, while all this recognition was pouring in, Murray was preparing to make the most of the success of *Snowbird*. In Toronto, Beckwith was putting a group together for the upcoming tour in support of the record. In the end, for most solo concerts, it consisted of drums, base, two horns, two guitarists, and a keyboard player, although this would be supplemented later by stringed and wind instruments for Las Vegas shows.

According to most reports the Canadian segment of the tour ran smoothly, although there were mixed reactions to its opening date at the Royal York Hotel's Imperial Room were Murray's bare feet caused a bit of a commotion. It was in the United States, reported Beckwith in *Maritime Music Greats: Fifty Years of Country and Folk* by Virginia Beaton and Stephen Peterson, that things got off to a rocky start. When they arrived in Chicago where they were to begin the tour, they discovered the club in question had recently endured a flood and remained full of water. Persevering, they went on with their sound check, then locked their instruments in the dressing room. When they returned a few hours before showtime, they discovered that everything was gone. "Beckwith's bass was stolen and sideman Lenny Breau's two guitars were gone. The record company took care of rentals and replacements, but as Beckwith recalls, it was an unpleasant reminder that they were in a big, tough business." Nonetheless, Murray was able to work with some big names in that decade, performing with the likes of Bruce Springsteen, Loggins and Messina, and Seals and Crofts.

On the more arduous side of Murray's life, now that *Snowbird* was such a runaway hit, was the apparently simple question of what to do next. Capitol arranged to have a meeting of the minds and released *Sing High Sing Low*. But in the United States, the song did not do all that well and remained on the American trade charts for only three weeks. In Canada, however, it was a big-seller.

With respect to Canada, Murray was still riding the crest of a receptive audience with a rather nationalistic aptitude for its music. And Murray seemed so frankly Canadian. While it was somewhat more difficult to crack successfully the barriers to stardom in the United States, Canadians were more forgiving of the halting steps forward on the part of Murray and her management after their initial realization that *Snowbird* had put them in the big leagues. "Anne Murray did become a star, as you well know, and she did it before anyone taught her the first things about stage presence and all the other little things that have traditionally gone into a star personality," wrote Jim Smith in *Sound* a few years afterwards. "Basically, I think that Canadians were so desperately in need of a star, some symbol of national identity (remember that this was just before the arrival of Canadian content requirements in radio programming and just after the Canadian Centennial that made everyone suddenly proud to be a Canadian), that, as a nation, we were willing to latch onto anything, no matter how little its merits, that had found acceptance by those arbiters of Canadian culture, the Americans."

Although Murray would ultimately prove this somewhat dismissive argument superficially inadequate by rising to superstardom later, there is nonetheless an element of truth in the assertion that a forgiving Canadian public gave her time to straighten out just where she was going musically. And Murray was well aware that she and many of those involved in her musical career were unprepared for the initial success of *Snowbird*. But several important steps were taken to correct the problem, though not before Murray underwent her own personal crisis in the wake of her initial success.

The formation of Balmur to optimize the opportunities her career would provide for her was one, complete with the insertion of Leonard Rambeau into the organization. The decision to take her on tour was another. But some of the other decisions had uncomfortable ramifications. A follow-up hit would not materialize for a protracted period of time and, in addition, there would be a Murray musical identity crisis. Ultimately, she would struggle to correct the image — exacerbated by her affiliation with country singer Glen Campbell and his successful television show — that she was just a country singer. At the end of this identify crisis she would emerge as one of the most successful crossover artists in music and her songs would run the gamut from rock to pop to folk to country.

In fact, writer David Livingstone, author of the 1981 authorized biography, *Anne Murray: The Story So Far*, would claim the year after *Snowbird* was not only the busiest in Murray's life, but "the worst." Characterized by frequent touring, more recording, a move to the twenty-second floor of a high-rise apartment on Balliol Street in Toronto, an appearance on the Grammys where she was nominated in two categories, and a hectic schedule of flying here and there despite her non-enjoyment of flight, her life prompted the Montreal *Gazette* to suggest "Anne Murray has to learn how to relax."

"I was a complete and total wreck," she told Livingstone. "A doctor who had gone to school with my brother gave me some very light tranquilizers, and I used them that week (Grammy week). That was that. I've never used them since, cause they put me right out of it."

And adding to the pressure was all that acclaim, an acclaim which found its focus in Springhill and in Nova Scotia generally where she had now become the local girl who makes good. A homecoming in July of 1971 was just one of the events which consumed her time and energy as Canada paid tribute to its new musical star.

But the touring and recording would continue. While Balmur handled all of her affairs, Murray turned her attention to the continued attempts to have another hit single in the United States and to sorting out her place in the new country music called "countrypolitan" which would change the tradition of country music forever, not only under Murray's tutelage, but with the assistance of names such as Dolly Parton, Olivia Newton-John, Kenny Rogers, and John Denver.

Nor would she be going it alone. Balmur represented a team of managers which a September 1973 article in *Toronto Life*, by Patrick Conlon, would call "Anne Murray's Maritime Mafia." The nickname wasn't new. But the approach to management was refreshing and loyal. To some, as far as Murray's career was concerned, it would eventually make all the difference.

Gene MacLellan, writer of Snowbird *and* Put Your Hand In The Hand, *performs with Anne Murray.*

CHAPTER FOUR

The Maritime Mafia

I'd get this close to the top and then back off. I'd get hot in the States then go off to England. Maybe I was running away. But it wasn't pleasant. It was awful. Most of the time I just wanted to quit.

— Anne Murray

◆ ◆ L ittle Miss Snowbird is surrounded by a canny clan of down-Easters who manage her the way Dalton Camp managed Bob Stanfield. Better, actually," trumpets the September 1973 issue of *Toronto Life* in a subtitle. Writer Patrick Conlon, hard on the heels of the real make-up of this Maritime family, pointed out that Toronto can appear a bit of a villain to those more used to the homespun ethic of Nova Scotia. And if Toronto is a villain, then Anne Murray is its dragon-slayer, a small-town Nova Scotian who made good in the cruel city and, as such, serves as an inspiration for all the other Maritimers who have come to Toronto to do well.

"Anne Murray. Our Annie. She gets up on the stage of the Royal York's Imperial Room and first thing she does is take off her shoes, just like down home. She's a big star now, our Annie. *Snowbird* was only the beginning. She owns a big house in Forest Hill now, and she's making millions and she's from Nova Scotia. She showed 'em, that's what she did," writes Conlon.

Murray herself claims to have come up with the term Maritime Mafia, and she claims to be sorry she did so. Her excuse? She wasn't feeling well when she approached the podium to accept a Juno Award and, under the weather, let the phrase slip unencumbered onto the airwaves. Whatever the origin of the nickname, Maritime Mafia has been a catchphrase to describe the clan of Maritimers who conduct Murray's various affairs, as far back as Bill Howell's 1972 *Maclean's* article which also focused on the cohesion Murray derived from the Maritime personalities who guide her. (The management group has at times also been dubbed Murray's Marauders.)

Who were the Maritime Mafia in the early 1970s? Brian Ahern, Bill Langstroth, Leonard Rambeau, accountant Lyman MacInnis, and lawyer David Matheson.

It was MacInnis who helped with the paperwork which created Balmur Ltd. At one time a partner in the prestigious international accounting firm of Coopers & Lybrand, he became financial advisor to Balmur and ultimately, in the wake of the death of Leonard Rambeau, picked up some of the slack at the company while Murray and the organization recovered from the loss of the respected personal manager. MacInnis did not, in the end, remain at the helm of Balmur but was replaced, in the role of personal manager, by Bruce Allen, manager of such notables as Bryan Adams. MacInnis didn't have the influence of Langstroth, Ahern, and Rambeau — his name does not form part of Balmur's letters as they do. (B, apparently is for Bill Langstroth, A is for Ahern, and L for Leonard Rambeau; the MUR is obvious).

MacInnis' job was to establish a financial safe zone for Murray because it was reported that she was determined to stop performing only when she reached the point when she wouldn't have to worry about money for the rest of her life. "Anne could quit this business tomorrow and she wouldn't be in hock. But, by the same token, if she quit this business tomorrow she'd be putting a lot of people out of work," said MacInnis.

"And if she died tomorrow, her beneficiaries would collect $1,000,000," observed Conlon. "The policy stipulates only that she isn't allowed to fly her own plane."

By way of anecdote, Conlon reported that the Maritimers enjoyed playing Rumoli to alleviate business from their minds, playing for pennies per hand. "One day, when Murray was carrying a cheque for $76,000 in her purse, she bid the alarming sum of 45 cents on a hand. MacInnis was genuinely shocked. He pounded his fist on the table, scattering drinks and cards, and said: 'There is no goddam Rumoli hand in the world that's worth 45 cents! I'm your financial advisor and I'm telling you not to do it.'

"Murray quickly whipped the cheque out and waved it under his nose. 'I've got $76,000,' she yelled, 'and if I want to bid a lousy 45 cents on this hand, I will!' "

David I. Matheson, the group's legal counsel, was born in Moncton and, according to Conlon, had already established a healthy law practice in Toronto when he was approached by MacInnis for the job. "He works closely with MacInnis through the labyrinthine tax laws that govern a performer who earns income on both sides of the border and across the Atlantic," wrote Conlon.

"There it is, in black and white, Mario Puzo could have written the story. Everyone on the regular Balmur staff, except for the receptionist, is a Maritimer. The Maritime Mafia, they're called, and with good reason. They think and act totally alike. They are satellites around the star, feeding her, serving her, enriching her. They know they're different and they close ranks against invasion. They have a language of their own and a code of honor that places friendship above business."

In the early 1970s, it was this group which tackled all the affairs of the woman who had become a star and was now concentrating on how to make that star shine even brighter, especially in the United States. They were intelligent, businesslike, extremely loyal to Murray herself and tightly-knit, adapting quickly to the business-oriented environment of Toronto. They also shared the common Maritime heritage of the drive and, as Murray herself once described it, the inferiority complex which the Maritimers sometimes feel when they look west towards Ontario and beyond.

"There's a close affinity among Maritimers that I can't describe," Matheson said in 1973, "but it's there and when you put together a nucleus of people who share the same feeling and the idea gets results, well, then, you're naturally proud to be part of it." And Matheson claimed much of the spirit was created by Murray herself. "There's a real warmth, a real excitement in this operation that's often lacking in a lawyer-client relationship. She'll tell us what she wants and expects and then it's discussed with the group and then we'll go off and get it."

Conlon observed: "And somehow, from the current that moves underneath his friendly words, I know I wouldn't like to be standing in the way."

Murray's management staff has always engendered a high regard in the music industry, not only in Canada but the United States. But a great deal of that can be attributed to Murray herself, a fact noted by Conlon in 1973. "Anne Murray isn't a puzzle anymore when she's read through the people who work with her," he said. "She has managed to command absolute loyalty and, yes, love from them all; both are strange commodities that Toronto has traditionally reserved for before nine and after five."

At the same time, he noted that the management team was extremely protective and there were barriers to prevent outsiders from reaching the musical star. "For right now, they sometimes strut across success like a platoon of stick figures, secure and powerful and curiously stripped of reality. Yet I know that, back home, they can sweat and scratch and put their feet up on the table. But they don't show Toronto that side of themselves, through fear or mistrust or simple dislike of the city."

Most enigmatic was Rambeau, a man described as a person who didn't give much away, totally dedicated to Murray and Balmur, a man who could talk about the woman and the company all night without ever letting anyone know how he truly feels about anything beyond his job. As Conlon remarked, "Like Murray, he has posted STOP signs all over his personality. He's considered to be one of the best personal managers in the business. He has an uncanny talent for timing, for announcing decisions at precisely the right moment to maximize their impact. Thus, he is wary of the press and distributes information like candy. He trusts few people and enjoys playing with rumors; he juggles them like oranges. His press releases are crisp, one-sheet bulletins mailed without folds in large envelopes."

The Maritime loyalty would go deeper in some respects for Murray in those years. At the Forest Hill home, it was reported, there was once a Corvette parked in the driveway, provided for her by General Motors for reasons of promotion, but when Volvo opened an assembly plant in Nova Scotia, two Volvos replaced the Corvette in the driveway.

More enigma. On the one hand, the connection of the Volvos, the property purchases in the Maritimes (at Peggy's Cove and in Prince Edward Island), homecomings and concert tours back home; on the other, a sense that Murray and her management had escaped from the Maritimes, were thankful to be at work and play in a larger universe. Murray herself would demonstrate both a love and a tedious boredom about back home, the way she would at times place her career second to her private life and express a disinterest in how well it was going, then suddenly push hard towards the superstardom she would eventually achieve. Apparently loyal to the Maritimes, she would also be dedicated to the "business" of being Anne Murray.

"She hasn't played Halifax since 1973, during what was then regarded as her homecoming tour," wrote George Anthony in the July 17, 1977 edition of *The Sunday Sun*. "That was four years ago.

Anne Murray can no longer afford to play the Maritimes. There simply isn't enough money there to make it a paying proposition. So the DuMaurier council decided to underwrite her appearance at the Rebecca Chon Auditorium, and she agreed to do it — the first time any artist has been booked for five consecutive nights at the Dalhousie Arts Centre, let alone sold out."

As writer Barry Conn Hughes observed in an early article about Murray, "For all her devotion to hard work, Anne seems to possess a healthy approach to her career. 'I've never taken it very seriously,' she told me. 'That would be lethal.' One illustration came in her last performance in Halifax. As the final strains of the haunting Randy Newman song *I'll Be Home* filled the hall, and tears welled in the eyes of the locals, I nipped backstage to observe Anne's own reaction. As she emerged in the wings, her eyes were dry, if tired. She walked quickly to her dressing room and mumbled, rather matter-of-factly, 'It's over. It's over.' "

And if Murray was a mystery, perhaps the most mysterious component of all in the early 1970s was Bill Langstroth. Conlon, perhaps unaware that Langstroth was romantically involved with Murray, described him as a question mark in the Maritime Mafia organization. "His official title is creative director, which gives him responsibility for all the promotional literature produced by the company. That includes programs, souvenir booklets, album jacket designs, the fan club newsletter and photography. He also directed her CBC specials until Balmur decided it would live without the corporation's possessive bickering. (Murray did not renew her CBC contract in 1973, although Langstroth insisted Murray and the CBC maintained a good relationship.) Now Langstroth seems to lurk in the background, busy with paper and wearing the crown of Discoverer.

"I once called Rambeau at home and Langstroth answered. He had just returned from putting Murray on a plane to an out-of-the-country concert. I asked him politely how she was. 'Aw, she's okay,' he said. 'When she steps out of line I just belt her in the chops.'

"He was kidding, of course. (Langstroth has been known forever for his sense of humor. In fact, Larry LeBlanc of *Billboard* maintains he is the funniest man he has ever met.) But the remark went whizzing by like an escaped prisoner. I never mentioned it to Rambeau because I knew it would cause an intense embarrassment. But I began to wonder about Langstroth. Did he want to prove he still controlled the star he discovered? Was he bitter? Was he tired of the Balmur armour and just being playful?

"Don't ask anyone at Balmur. Langstroth is another STOP sign."

And at the time he most certainly was. Married and with children by that marriage, no-one knew that Murray and Langstroth had a romantic interest which dated back to 1968. Conlon's report of the living arrangements at Murray's Forest Hill home, mentioned in passing, understates what Murray would later admit were the real reasons for which such a living arrangement was arrived at. "Rambeau, Langstroth and Anne's brother Bruce are permanent guests in the house, which Murray bought for $90,000 in late 1972."

But by the end of the 1980s, it was reported quite clearly that these living arrangements had had a romantic reason as well as others. "When Anne moved to Toronto in 1971 to be near the recording infrastructure she needed to develop her career, she masked the nature of her relationship with Bill by having manager Leonard Rambeau, her brother Bruce and others share a Forest Hill mansion with them," reports Elspeth Cameron in her September 1988 *Chatelaine* article about Murray. "Clever? You bet."

Why all the mystery? As Cameron conjectured, "By 1968, Anne Murray and Bill Langstroth were in love. Problem was, Langstroth was neither Roman Catholic nor free. Fifteen years older than Anne, he was Anglican and married with two small children. Anyway you looked at it, it was a messy situation. Not at all the sort of life a nice Catholic girl from Nova Scotia should be leading." Cameron wasn't reporting much that hadn't been known by that time, however. In an October 20, 1979 advertising supplement to *Billboard*, the romance was mentioned quite matter-of-factly in a feature devoted to the artist and the Maritimers who looked after her career.

"By 1968, however, she and Langstroth realized that business had become personal — 'by August of that year we were definitely, uh, you might say aware of each other' — and decided to concentrate on their off-camera relationship," the advertising supplement said. Langstroth and Murray would marry on her birthday, June 20, 1975 and go on to begin a family, William Jr., born August 31, 1976, and Dawn, born April 16, 1979.

The co-residence in Toronto of at least some members of the "Maritime Mafia" was analogous of the conflicts in Murray's own personality and underlined the close rapport she required of her management. A tightly knit group of Maritimers was exactly what she would require to put up the barriers to any investigation of her apparent enigma. Throughout most of her career, she has represented a conflicting sense of ideas and directions. Reportedly offhand about her career, she has tenaciously pursued it. Seeing the advantages of her girl-next-door image, she has staunchly encouraged it in the public eye and repelled any attempts by the media to cut beneath it to the harder edge which lurks beneath. Connected to what has been termed her "beloved Nova Scotia," she has purchased property there and returned for several days of high-school reunion celebration, yet permitted performance gaps there of several years when touring there would have not been financially profitable. She has decried others for using their names to sell commercial products, then turned around and promoted in a giant advertising campaign the merits of the Canadian Imperial Bank of Commerce. She remains stubbornly Canadian, in both residence and attitude, yet aggressively pursued American stardom. Refusing to perform in Las Vegas, alluding to its glitter, perhaps its fatuousness, she nonetheless relented when her terms were met and, in addition, used Vegas performances to define the extent of her success. Intent on leading a private life, she took on the most public of professions, singlemindedly pursued success yet refused television shows, concerts, and other career-developing projects because it did not fit into her plans for her family and her private interests.

It is possible a group of clannish Maritimers were the only individuals who could manage the affairs of someone like Anne Murray. Only they could juggle the conflicting personalities of the talented performer. In the wake of the success of *Snowbird* and the creation of Balmur Ltd. to manage her affairs, the "Maritime Mafia" was perhaps the only group that could put out the barriers and implement the wishes of a performer who did and did not want success and who was sometimes in conflict with her image.

Larry LeBlanc says Anne Murray has basically made all her own decisions where her career is concerned. Notwithstanding the expertise of her management and the respect it has in the music industry, it is Anne Murray who has steadfastly pursued her career and her private life and ensured that both have developed to her satisfaction, even when there seemed apparent inconsistencies and conflicts.

Murray's career, especially in the early days, presented a contrast between her wholesome image and the more truthful fact that she has always been in control of her own career. Although it was implied that her career was managed by people other than herself, while in truth the Maritime Mafia often protected her from the outside world, for the most part it was Murray herself who was in charge of it all along. As Richard Flohil put it in a profile in *Canadian Musician*, "The hidden key to Murray's considerable success can be found in the person of Leonard Rambeau, her long-time manager, friend, and combination Barnum and Svengali. Rambeau runs her management company, Balmur Ltd. in an easy and informal style — but he knows how to be tough when he has to be, and he knows how to keep the flak from Murray herself. They never fight ('although I do remember getting really pissed at him once for two minutes when he gave my phone number to someone he shouldn't have, and I told him not to do it again') and she takes part in all the major decision-making.

"Rambeau, in turn, says that Murray is the easiest person in the world to work with, but a tough one to change around once she has made up her mind. 'The fact is,' he says ruefully, 'that when she does make up her mind about something she's invariably right.' "

According to Larry LeBlanc, editor of *Billboard* in Toronto and author of a rather infamous *Maclean's* article on the star in 1974, Murray conducts her own affairs with strength and purpose, though image would have people believe otherwise. In short, she is a tough cookie. Leblanc even goes so far as to say that people who regularly disagree with her are not part of the organization very long.

Certainly she isn't above at least a gentle reproach of those who have moved on while her career has progressed. In Flohil's article, even Murray's initial producer and, more importantly, encouragement to tackle music professionally, Brian Ahern takes a slight poke, though not in Murray's own words as does the producer who followed him, Tom Catalano. "Her last two albums on Capitol were both produced by Jim Ed Norman, who followed Tom Catalano and Brian Ahern as her producers-in-residence. He is, she reports, 'simply the best producer anywhere for me.' Ahern, who worked on the first eight albums she made, was frequently disorganized, and liked working late into the night — Murray is not a 'night person' and occasionally resented the additional work made necessary by Ahern's casual way of doing things. Tom Catalano, who had produced a number of highly successful albums for Neil Diamond, was the exact opposite — 'too organized, almost sterile in his approach,' Murray recalls now. Worse, Catalano preferred to work in Los Angeles — he played a major role in picking material, and shipped it out to various arrangers, leaving Murray to come in and do the vocal tracks over material she couldn't identify with. 'There were times I felt that I could have stayed home in Toronto and phoned in the album,' she laughs."

This drive to succeed, to reach the top, to manipulate her career in that manner may go a long way to explaining why there have been a number of image changes over the years. From barefoot folksinger to wholesome girl next door to glitter, the image changes reflect a career which is regularly maintained even while it seems buffeted by the changeable trends of the times. The interesting fact, however, is that each image adjustment has stirred some level of controversy in the news media, as if fine turning one's career direction is somehow mutually exclusive with being "nice" or ethical. Certainly Murray would not equate herself with a person who drives her own career with unscrupulousness.

In fact, in the early years after the release of her first hit record, *Snowbird*, it was Murray who knew the time had come to regroup and examine where she was going. "I'd been working only for work's sake," she told Paul King in *Today*. "It all seemed to no avail. I'd go on the road for three months, play to 500 people in a 3,000-seat auditorium, then come home and have no money. It had all gone in 'overhead'.

"It was totally demoralizing. They just kept me working. Nothing was planned. There were no career moves happening. People didn't understand what I wanted; I was just sent out. My U.S. managers would phone and I wouldn't talk to them. I tried to avoid them like the plague. I thought we were on different sides because I was never consulted.

"But a lot of the trouble was my attitude. I'd get *this* close to the top and then back off. I'd get hot in the States and then go off to England. Maybe I was running away. But it wasn't pleasant. It was awful. Most of the time I just wanted to quit."

Larry LeBlanc knows well the kind of anger Murray can demonstrate if a profile pries beneath the image to get at her other side. He makes it quite clear that Murray did not speak to him for more than five years after *Maclean's* printed his article "The Flip Side of Anne Murray" in November of 1974. Leonard Rambeau was a little more forgiving. About a year after the article came out, he apologized to LeBlanc for Murray's reaction to the piece. The image conflict with the real person is not an uncommon characteristic for entertainers. Indeed, comedians and impressionists have used it as fodder for spoofs for years. LeBlanc's article outlines the details of an Anne Murray performance in Kansas City, Missouri, relating how nervous she is before she goes onstage, from "nervous pees" to prowling the narrow cement block corridor behind the stage. "She was friendly but unsmiling to those who came up to her, remaining aloof and somewhat stern," wrote LeBlanc. " 'Before I go on stage,' she had told me, 'I'm completely preoccupied. I yawn a lot. I have my usual nervous pees. When I talk to people I don't give them the attention they deserve. The only thing I think about is what I'm going to do out there. I just go inside myself.' "

Despite a performance which demonstrated her sureness on stage and her ability to win over an audience, there were a couple of incidents during the show and afterwards which unsettled her and revealed that Murray can demonstrate some temper. "After the encores she swept into the windowless dressing room, edgy looking, uptight." LeBlanc reported, "She started firing questions at anyone in sight, and a feeling of embarrassment coated the musty air. Skip Beckwith, the band's leader, rolled his eyes in recognition of this show of hostility. 'Andy,' he called over to drummer Andy Cree, 'she wants to see you.' Beckwith jerked his thumb in the direction of the dressing room and Cree followed it. Anne blasted him harshly for the loudness of his drumming. He listened but said nothing.

" 'Hell,' Cree said later to Beckwith. 'I thought it sounded great out there.'

" 'It was okay. She just needed something to bitch about.'

"Skip and Anne talked about the noise. 'We always play at that level,' argued Skip.

" 'Well,' she shot back, 'during *Robbie's Song* if Miles [the group's sound technician] had been on stage I would have punched him in the head.' "

Most of all, the incident seemed to be less with the performance than the rigors of being on tour and being a rising star with aggressive fans who sometimes instigated frightening encounters. The one incident took place during the performance itself. "Halfway through, a handsome youth in a styled denim suit slipped out of the audience, walked up and presented Anne with a dozen long-stemmed roses. He was rather good-looking, short-cropped hair, of course, but nice looking still and when he made the motion to present Anne with the gift, she stooped as if to kiss him on the lips. He said something though, and Anne turned away awkwardly, abruptly, and her lips barely touched his cheek."

Next day Murray herself explained what had happened. " 'You know that guy who came on stage last night with the flowers?' she said to the band. 'It was a girl. I went to kiss him full on the lips but just then he said something and instead I kissed him on the cheek. Then I noticed he had a smooth face like mine.' "

LeBlanc also related an encounter between Murray and a tough female fan from whom Murray escaped by leaping sideways into an elevator. The fan had wanted her to come down to the bar for a drink.

The article went on to outline Murray's feelings about the music business. "Anne also relies on her Toronto partners (particularly Rambeau) to shield her from what she calls the 'nitty-gritty facts' of the business — 'you know, the real dirt. I'm a little bit too sensitive about some things. Like I don't want to know that there's money being paid to people to play a performer's records, if that indeed is true' (her staff insists that in her case it's not). 'I don't want to know what promoters have to do to paper a house, so that when a performer comes out on stage the house is three-quarters full, rather than having 200 people there. I'm aware of all these things. But I just don't always want to be told.' The cold facts about the entertainment business coming from Anne's lips sound too . . . too, well, *unwholesome* for the image we have built up of her," concludes LeBlanc.

The *Maclean's* piece concludes with the dichotomy between success and privacy which seems to forever daunt Murray's life. "After touring four dates with her — Rochester, Detroit, Columbus and Kansas City — I became very aware that privacy is the one priority she places almost as high as making it. But it's a peculiar privacy: some things are okay to talk about, others not. You don't, for instance, bring up her long personal association with Bill Langstroth. And you cannot determine what she's worth, though she's obviously wealthy on paper at least (with her best-selling records, an upcoming contract rumored to be worth a couple of million dollars or so, and impressive land holdings in the Maritimes which include a motel, a share of a trailer park and land around Peggy's Cove). In return for her pressing ambition she has lost the freedom to live an ordinary life; she won't go anywhere in public anymore, not to a restaurant, not even to a drugstore. She won't trust sunglasses because someone once recognized her by her smile.

"But that's success, and she'll do all she can to protect what privacy she has left. The most important consideration right now is to make it very, very big in the United States. And if that means giving up her image as queen of the high school prom, that's just part of the price she has to pay."

As LeBlanc so frankly points out, audiences choose their stars, stars don't choose their audiences, and this simple but sometimes forgotten fact is at the bottom of any conflict between image and living a private life. In Murray's case, Canadians embraced her down-home image in the period after *Snowbird* took her to the top and, in Canada, this image still persists. Perhaps LeBlanc only explained half of it. Audiences not only pick their stars but decide who they are. Reality doesn't enter into it. Then, caught in the maelstrom of success, the artist is tugged along inside the confines of the image, earning the income which often goes along with it, trapped by the superficiality.

Murray, as much as any other musical star, has had to suffer inside this apparent cocoon. Murray, as much as any other artist, has sometimes resisted the unshakeable truth that there is a public possession component to earning your generous living in the public eye. And when you try to change your image, perhaps bring a little more candor into it, the audience is going to resist. In a sense, it owns the star. It sets the terms.

"She became our permanent high school sweetheart," wrote LeBlanc. "This image was groomed by her staff, who were largely inexperienced themselves, and she soon found it impossible to shake. People loved her for the *goodness* she projected on *Singalong Jubilee*, *Let's Go* and her specials. In some ways, she became part of the Canadian nationalism movement. Just as many Canadians are against foreign investment *on principle*, without any clear idea of what resources are being taken over by whom, many Canadians love Anne Murray *on principle*, without knowing or even caring much about her music."

As the middle of the 1970s decade approached, Anne Murray was suffering an identity crisis. The woman who had rocketed to international stardom on the strength of a million-selling Gene MacLellan single remained reluctant and ambitious at the same time, wanted a private family life and career at the same time, was stuck with a homegrown image which, though profitable, was vapidly incomplete.

Her management's assignment was to sort through these apparent conflicts and guide Anne Murray into the next phase of her career. There would be a bleak period of adjustment but ultimately they would succeed.

Brian Ahern produced 10 albums by Anne Murray before moving to California where he formed his own production company and married Emmylou Harris.

Mentor, friend, and manager Leonard Rambeau poses with Anne Murray and Paul White, who signed her to Capitol Records.

Lyman MacInnis, Anne Murray's business manager since 1971, took over from Leonard Rambeau after his death in 1995 and was replaced before the end of the year by Bruce Allen who also manages Bryan Adams.

Bill Langstroth discovered Anne Murray in 1964.
They were married in 1975.

CHAPTER FIVE

This Way Is My Way

People come up and say, "We don't like you since you've changed." I say I haven't changed. They say they've changed me. What a pile of bullshit. — Anne Murray

In the years which followed the runaway success of *Snowbird*, Murray nearly gave up the music business. According to Larry LeBlanc she was fed up with it. And considering that Murray had been somewhat reluctant to even turn to music full time in the early days, the long lapse which immediately followed the initial success brought on by *Snowbird* seemed more than enough of an excuse to pack it all in. Although sales of singles released after *Snowbird* did well in Canada, the lucrative and star-shaping market of the United States did not respond. Murray became convinced that she was a one-hit wonder. And the lack of response was doubly hard to take because of all the effort which had gone into the recording sessions which followed the rise of her personal star. (Throughout her entire career, Murray would have the reputation as the consummate professional in the recording studio, always arriving with her voice in shape, even in the morning when some are not prepared for recording.)

As Jim Smith at *Sound* put it, "With the success of *Snowbird* behind her, it seemed that nothing could cool the ardor of her Canadian following. At the same time, though, her records weren't all smash hits. The boys at Capitol Records, who have been handling her career since the *Snowbird* days, advised against release of *Put Your Hand In The Hand* — and it turned out to be the one song that could have established her as a major international star. Meanwhile, the records she was releasing were being played, but they weren't selling like we all believed."

Indeed, her recording output at the time was immense. After the release of the album SNOWBIRD in 1970 and prior to the release of DANNY'S SONG in 1973, there were the albums HONEY, WHEAT & LAUGHTER, STRAIGHT, CLEAN & SIMPLE, TALK IT OVER IN THE MORNING, her joint effort with Glen Campbell, and ANNIE.

In an interview later put out in a Capitol Records promotional package, Murray was asked at the time if ANNIE was her favorite album. "Yes. There are things I would change on it. There are mixes. I didn't sing as well on the album as I should have. I'm not sure of the reasons for it. There are a couple of tunes that I would redo the voices on if I had the chance. And Brian would remix a couple of songs if he ever got the chance. I listened to it for the first time in a long time the other night. I listened to the DANNY'S SONG album and the ANNIE album and the Arc album. I hadn't listened to that in about three years. That is incredible. That is really incredible to listen to that. It sounds like we are both in kindergarten doing a record. I just laughed. You can hear the potential but it sure needed a lot of working on. I like the DANNY'S SONG album too. I can't decide between the two. I think ANNIE, material-wise, is my favorite. It was all ours. The only ones that weren't were *Beautiful* by Carole King and the other a Paul Anka tune, but the rest of it was all new. That is really starting from the ground up and doing it all on your own. That is the greatest satisfaction in the whole world."

From the standpoint of single releases, there had been, in the wake of *Snowbird, Sing High, Sing Low, A Stranger In My Place, It Takes Time, Talk It Over In The Morning, I Say A Little Prayer/By The Time I Get To Phoenix* (with Glen Campbell), Gord Lightfoot's *Cotton Jenny*, and *Robbie's Song For Jesus*. As Larry LeBlanc pointed out in 1974, after *Danny's Song* and *Love Song* had become hits, "Anne Murray is no longer in the same space she was in the days when *Snowbird* was her big song. Gone is the air of innocence. There's been a subtle but visible drift away, a departure brought on by five years propped up on pillows against carbon-copied Holiday Inn headboards, watching one crummy television show after another. It's made her grow up . . . and she's mature enough now, at 29, to make her own decisions. She's a bit of a phenomenon in that she's now come around twice, after close to two years in show business limbo she's a star *again*, proving that *Snowbird* was no fluke.

"Anne has made some big changes this past year, some of which have hurt old fans. Practically every entertainment publication on the continent has run a story on the Remaking of Anne Murray's Image; and the accolades — in some cases the blame — have been laid mostly with her new American managers Shep Gordon and Allan Strale, hardly ever with Anne herself, which is where they should have gone. Snuffling Canada couldn't bring itself to believe that the real push to make it big in the United States came from Anne herself and her Canadian advisers, not from the two New Yorkers."

But both writers, LeBlanc and Smith, were writing in 1974 and Murray herself would later talk about a span of time which stretched into 1975. In *her* mind, having another hit record in Kenny Loggins' *Danny's Song* was only a partial solution to the problems which plagued her in the period following *Snowbird*'s surprise success.

There was a side to her which remained reluctant where the music business was concerned. And she was having as much trouble with her image as anyone else was, disliking the country label with which she had been tagged. But image seemed to be at the core of the general period of frustration in a larger sense. Should she or should she not chase after the lucrative American market. And would it be image-appropriate to pursue her goal of financial independence in that dreaded American marketplace? With it well reported that she had declined invitations to live in Los Angeles in favor of remaining in Canada, how would it look if she changed her mind? (She never has, perhaps only because she ultimately didn't have to.) In addition, Murray had other priorities. She felt she was missing out on those other aspects of life such as marriage and having a family.

As she told Bob Allen, "There were times when I just couldn't go on. It happened to me twice. The year after 'Snowbird' I didn't know what I was doing. It was a matter of stopping and saying, 'Look, I don't *have* to do anything.' Then again in 1975 I just said, 'Look, I just don't see any point to this.' "

In the wake of *Snowbird*, the rather gleeful what-do-we-do-now had become the truly *confusing* what-do-we-do-now. The *Snowbird* magic all but evaporated, her career dribbling away with cool U.S. reception, playing clubs to small audiences in the United States, dismissed by the press as a one-hit wonder, overexposed in her arrangement with Glen Campbell as just a country singer, overexposed in another way in Canada, due in part to her contract with the CBC. In the United States, however, it was *under*exposure which was stalling her career.

Bit by bit, she began to sort through the confusion in an attempt to decide what to do, as Larry LeBlanc reports. "Her U.S. manager, Nick Sevano (who also handles Glen Campbell), and her booking agent, the William Morris Agency, were holding her to the choking confines of the country music charts and molding her into the Liza Minelli/Roberta Flack Las Vegas nightclub style. They told her it was impossible for her to perform on the college circuits (where the good concert money is) or even in the smaller, big-city halls. They claimed she just wasn't wanted. Her singles were flopping outside Canada, and her producer, Brian Ahern, and Anne herself were reluctant to change from the familiar Anne Murray sound, even though it was shimmering dangerously close to schmaltz. Her options soon became clear: either settle in to being a minor Canadian star, perhaps with a comfortable network television series, or else roll back the stone from the tomb and step out.

" 'I was almost to the point of quitting . . . and yet I wasn't,' she recalls. 'There were just enough people around to encourage me. All I could think about was that I was a one-hit wonder. I figured that must be it because it had happened so many times before. I also knew I had the talent. The challenge was out there because I had had a taste of it and I felt deep down it could be done. But I needed help.' "

Help came from Capital Records, which put extra money and time into *Danny's Song*. For some, it was the true long-awaited follow up to *Snowbird*. "Still," said LeBlanc, "when the record took off, no concert dates in the U.S. followed, and she wanted that more than anything else, even though she claims to despise traveling."

In the end, Murray fired Nick Sevano and the William Morris Agency and, late in 1973, she and her management in Toronto asked Shep Gordon and Allan Strale to take a crack at opening up the American market. It seemed an unusual choice on the surface. Gordon and Strale were best known for their work with a Phoenix youth named Vincent Fournier whom they had transformed into Alice Cooper, known for the ostentatious horror of his stage show. Nonetheless, Gordon pitched in to try to correct the downturn in interest in Murray since *Snowbird* and, with the efforts of a veteran public relations man named Ron Grevatt, Murray soon turned up in *Time, Newsweek, Performance, National Observer, Seventeen*, and a variety of entertainment magazines such as *Rolling Stone, Creem*, and *Zoo World*. As well, she made appearances on *The Merv Griffin*

Show, *Midnight Special*, an *Englebert Humperdinck Special*, the *Tonight Show*, and a special with the rock group Chicago.

In Canada, of course, the sudden turn of events sent shock waves throughout her legions of fans. "People come up and say, 'We don't like you since you've changed.' I say I haven't changed. They say *they've* changed me. What a pile of bullshit," said Murray.

"The management I've had in the past wasn't always working for me," she said then. "I was told for two years that there was no demand whatsoever for me in the States, so I was really doing nothing at all there. But when I went to Shep, he put me on the road in August and I played to packed houses everywhere in the States from then until December 2nd. So there is a demand — but I was being told there wasn't.

"Shep has a different impression of what I should be doing. He has me working clubs like the Cellar Door in Washington, D.C., which are prestigious clubs and they're fun to do because they're small and intimate and warm. If I had gone along the way I was going, I probably would be playing places like the Cocoanut Grove. I don't think that I'm the type of singer who should be playing at the Cocoanut Grove.

"We have to keep working at building a career for me in the States. I think I could have established a career for myself in the States when *Snowbird* was so successful. But I was committed to quite a few television shows in Canada for that year and, with all those television shows, I didn't have time for the States. Now I know that that was too bad."

As for the progress of *Danny's Song*, the song made both pop and country upperchart levels as did the LP of that title issued in April 1973. Other singles on both pop and country charts in 1973 included *What About Me, Send A Little Love My Way*, and *Love Song*. The latter song was on the chart lists from late 1973 into early 1974 and, when Capitol issued another LP in February 1974, LOVE SONG, it too also did very well. Interestingly enough, there were singles in that period that made only the pop chart lists, songs like *You Won't See Me, Just One Look*, and *Day Tripper*. All came out in 1974, a banner year in that it provided Murray with two major country chart hits, *He Thinks I Don't Care*, which rose to number one, and *Son Of A Rotten Gambler*, which made the country top five. Two more albums were released that year as well, COUNTRY in August and HIGHLY PRIZED POSSESSION in November.

But, in all of this, who was the real Anne Murray? George Anthony asked in *Chatelaine* early in 1975 how she kept that level head. "It was such a change in focus," said Murray. "When I was teaching high school kids phys-ed — how to play basketball — I put all the focus on them. Then all of a sudden all that focus was turned in on me. It took me almost two years to adjust to that." According to Anthony, Murray was not impressed with Hollywood people and said so. "They live showbiz every day of their lives. They've got to go to an opening every night, they're frantic about getting their picture taken with somebody who may be important now or later. They eat and sleep it, and it makes me very uncomfortable. I've got to get away from it. My father was a doctor, but when he came home from the hospital we didn't hear about it. He got away from it, he led a normal existence. He had a private life. I intend to have one, too."

But if Murray was seeking a private life, Shep Gordon and company were intent on making it as public as possible. Part of the image turnaround, it appeared, was to make Anne Murray "hip." Which was why when Murray debuted at the prestigious Troubador in Los Angeles on Thanksgiving in November of 1973, Gordon took the opportunity to arrange for a photograph of Murray with John Lennon, Harry Nilsson, Alice Cooper, and former Monkee Mickey Dolenz, making it look like an accident, but setting it up just the same, a photograph which did the rounds of the news media in style. (It's one of the photos on display in the Anne Murray Centre, by the way.)

The event took place in the middle of a gala party dedicated to the American Thanksgiving. It was reputed to cost $35,000 and, reportedly, that cost was divided between Balmur and Capitol, the former chipping in ten grand, the latter picking up the remaining $25,000. On the menu? About 200 gallons of wine and approximately 300 pounds of turkey. Murray, herself, was called upon to emerge from a giant wooden turkey to begin to entertain.

A rather hackneyed news release about the event from Alive Enterprises Inc., the Shep Gordon management company, in New

York, provided the best picture: "LOS ANGELES — It was a traditional Thanksgiving dinner from start to finish as the Anne Murray Show opened at Doug Weston's Troubador last Wednesday evening. The festivities started more than a week prior as Capitol page Calvin Smith put on his plumage and kazooed and tap-danced his way around the streets of Hollywood hand-delivering the holiday message, 'Hear Ye! Hear Ye! Capitol Records hereby decrees that to celebrate the olde and tyme-honoured tradition of Thanksgiving your presence is most cordially requested at a sumptuous feaste of victuals, wines and spirits to be given in honour of the faire and beauteous Lady Anne Murray.' The transformation in the Troubador was obvious from the start as guests were greeted at the door by two colonial foot soldiers, complete with knickers and spats. Pochohantas then personally received all of the guests and presented them with age-old boxes of snuff and a copy of Anne's latest single, 'Love Song.' Everyone was then asked to sign a parchment scroll to attest to their presence to the fete. As they entered, guests passed by portraits of Anne drawn by the third grade class of the Pinecrest Grammar School here in Los Angeles.

"The situation inside was much the same as Indians danced around hooping [sic] and hollering, pilgrims looked fashionably grim and proper, and minstrels sang and played a variety of instruments. The tables overflowed with a variety of nuts, pies, flowers and platters of fresh fruit. In the patriotic tradition of the long honored holiday, Betsy Ross sat in one corner of the room and meticulously sewed her flag. Even the stage could not escape the spirit of the evening. Jim Newton had transformed the normally bare Troubador stage into a colorful double-fanned turkey. Newton has had a successful career in designing television and stage sets and is best known in the music world for his involvement in designing the sets for Neil Diamond's Winter Garden appearances in New York and the set for Alice Cooper's Billion Dollar Babies show.

"With much vocal fanfare, a dozen Indians and pilgrims heralded the serving of the Thanksgiving feast. The meal, prepared by Poppy of the Great American Food and Beverage Corporation, included five 35-pound turkeys, twelve 15-pound turkeys, 150 turkey drum sticks, 35 turkey hindquarters, 600 jumbo spare ribs,

100 pounds of white sliced turkey, 100 pounds of sliced Danish ham, 100 pounds of sweet potatoes, 6 cases of fresh corn, 75 loaves of seasoned stuffing bread, 500 pounds of fresh fruit from six countries, 50 assorted pies, 100 pounds of mixed nuts, 2 cases of giant olives, 20 loaves of corn bread, 10 giant loves of pumpernickel bread, 200 gallons of wine and egg nog and 20 gallons of assorted sauces. Among the celebrities who joined the Lady Anne Murray for this Thanksgiving celebration were John Lennon, Harry Nilsson, Mickey Dolenz, Helen Reddy, Jesus Christ Superstar Ted Neeley and Alice Cooper.

"After much wining, dining and joviality the evening was climaxed by the performance of Anne Murray. Anne was joined by her back-up band, Richard, and 8 tuxedoed string players. According to Doug Weston, owner of the club, 'This was one of the finest nights in the long history of the Troubador.' Commenting on the success of the affair, Anne's manager, Shep Gordon, was quoted as saying, 'Nothing would have been possible without the fantastic cooperation we received from Capitol.' "

If this seems rather lavish and glitzy, especially to Canadians, it seemed to fit right in with the Murray makeover which included a new $50,000 wardrobe dedicated to the new image. And there was no quarreling with the success of the Shep Gordon initiative. The "spontaneous" photograph with Lennon *et al* found its way into a seemingly endless array of news media, so much so that those which did not print the photograph launched self-congratulatory stories about the fact.

And most significant of all, critics and writers began to promote her sex appeal. Gone was the barefoot girl next door image. There were those who decided her appeal fell just short of the Brigit Bardot of song. Most famous of all of these tributes to her sexuality was that penned by a rather enthused American critic, Lester Bangs, who panted: "Anne Murray is God's gift to the male race. You may think she's a middling milquetoast marianne schoolteacher Parcheesi player with oldmaid nodes on her nips, but you gotta nother think coming Bud . . . I know what I want: I wanna hold hands. I wanna bill and coo sweet nuttins in her well-formed Canadian ear. Then, while I'm reducing her to a quivering mass of erogenized helplessness, I'll check out the rest of her to see if this soiree is worth pursuing further . . . I know she's gonna be great because all Canadian babes are tops, it's in their bloodlines and the way they raise em up thar."

Murray took it in stride. "I thought it was great. I got a big charge out of that. Anybody can sit down and write down their fantasies. He seems to be a fan, and if that's the way he feels about me, great. It certainly turned a few heads around."

The media continued to sort through the implications of the image change and began to seek out the *real* Anne Murray. Was the down home girl really a hipster in disguise or was the newly revitalized hipster really a down home girl under all that hype?

"I personally haven't done anything to change in any way," said Murray. "I suppose if you talk to Shep, he'll tell you these are the things we're doing, but I'm just doing the same things I always did. The only difference is that I'm a few years older and I finally have people who are getting off their asses and doing something constructive for me," she told writer Bob Dunne in *Beetle*.

Dunne, in an offhand way, probably addressed the real issue surrounding performers such as Murray, the fact that management keeps a close eye on image and will do whatever it can to manipulate it to the advantage of the performer. "But Anne's career depends also on steering the public's focus away from certain angles as much as it depends on playing up others."

Even back home in Canada, the media was scratching its head and trying to sort through the puzzle. Marci McDonald, in *The Toronto Star*, took a crack at it, complete with the aforementioned photo with Alice Cooper and the others nestled into the top right-hand corner. "Take one apple-cheeked, apple-pie, all-Canadian girl next door . . . And scrap her. Just, zap, spend a fortune trying to stamp her out of all memory," wrote McDonald. "Then bring on the image-makers and add a $50,000 new wardrobe of silk, and satin funky chic, cool the twangy guitars, heat up the backstreet, background soul, stir up a $35,000 gala underground coming-out party complete with 200 gallons of wine, 300 pounds of turkey and hand-delivered scroll invitations from kazoo-playing pages dressed up as pilgrims to a guest list that reads like the radical chic of Who's Who in rock 'n' roll, sprinkle in a snapshot of John Lennon and a salty onstage three-letter word or four, bring it all to a boil on a 41-city, cross-continent concert blitz, and what have you got?"

"I was desperate, absolutely desperate," said Murray. "I just had to get away from the whole barefoot thing — I got stuck with an image that was hurting me. It was all garbage anyway. I was so sick of that girl next door."

Which wasn't all she was sick of.

"I just got sick of looking like I was riding on Glen Campbell's coattails. I was doing a tour of England with Glen last spring for like $10,000 — terrible money — and one day in the back of the limousine Glen said something about a tour together for the whole summer. And I said, 'Glen, do you know what I'm doing now is an insult?' He just went nuts when he found out what I was being paid and offered me a lot of money.

"But I said, 'Glen, there's no way I can go out with you again. I've gotta get my own thing together.' "

As cynical as it sounds, however, Murray didn't seem confused about the fact that her image was simply that, *image*.

"You know," she said candidly, "everytime I read about how I've gone hip, I laugh. Because I'm the same person who likes to watch the hockey game, who doesn't have time for a social life and, believe me, now with this image thing, it would be to my advantage to say I'm having an affair with a married man even if I'm not. But suddenly I'm associated with Alice Cooper, I'm having my picture taken with John Lennon, I've got some clothes and I'm hip. It's funny. But that's what the business is all about."

To Murray, it seemed to be a question not only of image but of growing up. Certainly it was all image and repackaging, but there was an element of developing a less shy and retiring character, of approaching her career more aggressively and directly. Previously, once she had gotten over her initial reluctance, in the pre-*Snowbird* days, she had demonstrated that she was intent on handling her affairs her way, but this had been packaged into the background. Now, glitzy image aside, *hipness* aside, Murray was going to come out of herself and tell it like it was.

"I was very shy when I first started in the business and didn't say much of anything. I figure now that if I had been familiar with the workings of the industry then, I might have spoken up and mouthed some opinions. But I didn't have any then. So people naturally assumed that I was just a dizzy blonde or something. Then of course I did the Glen Campbell show which really helped my career a lot but also reinforced that stereotype."

And Murray began to give her opinions. "If you put out three things in a row that sound even remotely similar, people automatically turn off. If they don't continue to listen to you, then they'll never know that you've changed. I can see a lot of people doing that with the Carpenters. They've put out one thing after another that sounded exactly the same, and I suppose that people could have said that about me. But if they'd listened to the last couple of albums, but by that time I guess they wouldn't anyway . . . but if they'd listened, they'd have seen that there was more there than what they hear on the AM radio, but that's been the case all along. But the Carpenters never even attempted to get out of that."

Murray was now outspoken, so much so that Britain's *Melody Maker* observed the difference. Writer Cole Irwin said in April of 1975, "Anne Murray, darling of Canada, snowbird, creator of ten albums and Grammy award winner, is quite a character. Rugged and outspoken, she could quite easily be reincarnated in another life as a lumberjack.

"There we were, all believing that Anne Murray was one of those sweet coo-ing country type singers, all sweetness and light and instantly acceptable to Radio Two. Yet here she is — frizzy blonde hair, jeans and open-necked shirt — littering the interview with a few four letter words and making a mockery of her popular public image. The type of person you'd be in two minds about taking home to mother."

Irwin noted that she wasn't over-modest either, despite the five-year gap between *Snowbird*'s arrival on the charts, her only British hit at the time, and his interview with her.

"I'm a great singer. I know this. I no longer have to be immodest about it or anything. I know that it's true," she said.

Not only were there opinions and a non-self-effacing approach to her music, but Murray had some blunt remarks about her then feud with fellow Canadian Terry Jacks. Reports said that the two began sniping at one another in the press after Jacks complained that Murray's publicity — claiming she was the first Canadian woman to get a gold disc — was false in view of the fact that, instead, it was his wife, Susan, for the Poppy Family's hit *Which Way You Going, Billy?*.

"For some reason he says I'm stupid for putting my money back into my company and developing other Canadian talent, whereas he takes his money and sorts it away. He doesn't have any people around him and I have people around me to handle things. *Seasons In The Sun* and nine million records later he's rich."

Murray expressed her ambivalence about the music business and what was wrong with being categorized as well. "Categories are stupid. The only categories should be good and bad. I know most of my hits have been ballads, like *Love Song*, *Danny's Song*, *Snowbird* and then *You Won't See Me*, which I suppose you could call rock 'n' roll. It's not Bachman Turner Overdrive, it's not Black Sabbath, but it's a kind of rock 'n' roll.

"I don't think you have to totally commit yourself to the business. Perhaps you do to become a Frank Sinatra or even a Helen Reddy, who is a giant in the United States. I don't hate her husband but everybody I've ever talked to does. He doesn't make too many friends but he's made Helen Reddy the biggest thing in the United States and to him that's the most important thing. My priorities are in a different place. I would rather have friends and never make it to the very top. I used to think that singing for a living would be such a lark — imagine doing something that comes so naturally and getting paid for it — but I've learned. There's so much politics. I don't have the buffers I once had. For two years I didn't know what went on on the road, in record companies, all the garbage that goes down, all the grease that goes down . . . but now I've seen it all. And I'm glad I have because you can only be insulated or protected for so long unless you're really stupid."

Having recently won a Grammy as top country singer, something she termed at the time as the highlight of her career, she was pragmatic about not being nominated in the pop category as she had been the year before, because no one had had a chance alongside Olivia Newton John.

"I don't care what they call me as long as they give me a Grammy," she said. "Y'know how they take a reaction shot in the audience when they announce the name of the winner? All they got were my heels running up to get that Grammy. People talk a lot of politics are involved and all that . . . and I think the fact that Elton John has had a year like he's just had this year and didn't win an American Music award or a Grammy or anything like that, that's ludicrous. So there's something wrong. I think what they try to do is get at as many people as they feel deserve awards and contribute to the music industry. I just can't imagine that Elton John didn't win a Grammy, but he didn't. Stevie Wonder always wins the awards, which he deserves, but Elton should have won something. He's so talented. I'm a really big fan of his. There's a guy who can sing anything he wants to sing. It's like Harry Nilsson who'll put out a masterpiece like *Without You* and then he'll put out something that's just s— and he's just laughing. And there are all those idiots out there buying that. That's part of the business."

Murray, at the time, admitted that it was a comparatively recent development for her to have so much confidence. "It's only in the last six months to eight months I've come out of my shell. I wouldn't move from hotels. I guess it was because of Canada. I couldn't go to the grocery store unless I signed fifty autographs. I thought that was an invasion of privacy. Not that I wasn't complimented, but I wanted to put a bag over my head, and I became a recluse."

If there was a new image for Anne Murray by the mid-1970s, there was also apparently a new Anne Murray. Indeed, she would continue to demonstrate her new confidence, her opinions, and an apparent cynicism about the music business for years to come. At the same time, however, the conflict between public and private life would continue to motivate her actions. She would become familiar with the negative aspects of being a star and would begin even more fiercely to defend her privacy. And through it all, the role of image and the media would be the football kicked back and forth between Murray the private person and Murray the performer, as LeBlanc noted: "But anyone who has known Anne for long is aware that she sometimes does use strong language. She sometimes drinks beer from the bottle, too. And smokes cigarettes, though never on television where the public might see. (A habit she has since given up.) But she was unable to convince the Canadian press that she hadn't changed overnight.

" 'The whole thing was a laugh because I was prepared for it," she says. "I knew exactly why they were coming [the reporters who showed up for a morning-long press conference at Toronto's Hyatt Regency] and I said okay, I can go in there and tell them, 'Oh, yes, my image has really changed and I'm not doing this or that anymore . . .' Mind you, I was honest with everyone. I said, 'Look, I'm no different than I was two years ago. I have some new clothes, but other than that . . .' and they took it from there.

" 'It's so ridiculous. You play games with the media. You tell them you haven't changed but their article has to be about the image. That's what they've been sent to find out. They end up writing something with an angle. They'll say, 'Oh, yes, definite differences in attitude, etc., etc.' They'll rationalize it in their own minds. There are certain people I consider to be bright and I can carry on a fairly intelligent conversation with. If I can do that with the press then I'll do it. But if they're going to niggly-piggly their way into me and what I am then I'll just shut them off. There are asses in the business that I will have nothing to do with. I never ask people about their private life. I don't think it's necessary to talk about that.' "

And as Bob Dunne commented, "And so the struggle to manipulate the media, placing Anne in a favorable light, continues. Leonard Rambeau attempts to shield her from bad press. Shep Gordon tries to arrange good press. Anne Murray, the centre of it all, acts as if she couldn't really care less."

"I haven't changed at all," she says for the last time. "I've always been this way."

The now famous photograph of Anne Murray at the Troubador in Los Angeles in 1973 with John Lennon, Harry Nilsson, Alice Cooper, and Mickey Dolenz.

*Anne poses with
Kenny Loggins who
wrote "Danny's Song"
and "Love Song."*

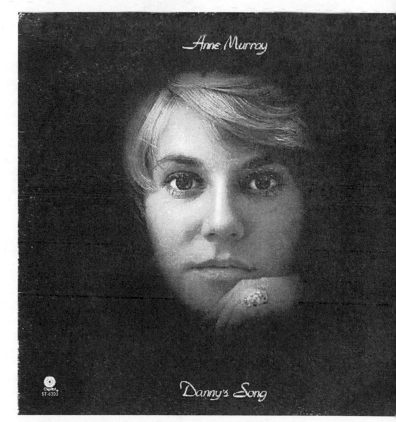

Anne's star appears on Hollywood Boulevard.

Anne Murray has won so many Juno awards since 1971 that media pundits have quipped the awards should be renamed the "Annies."

Anne is inducted into the Country Music Hall of Fame in Nashville.

Sporting a fashionable fur coat and sun glasses during a trip to the Canadian North.

Hamming it up with Mike Douglas and Jim Nabors during a Mike Douglas Show.

CHAPTER SIX

You Won't See Me

I intended to have a private life.
— Anne Murray

I n 1975 Anne Murray said, "Look, I just don't see any point to any of this."

It was a general statement but perhaps defined a final assessment on her part that she had better take a look at her life. Murray was about to take steps that would be more personal in nature, would seek to fulfil the needs of the more private aspect of her life and, at the same time, provide a hiatus from stardom. By the end of the year, she would be intent on living a meaningful private life, would be concerned about and committed to starting a family. She would also accept changes in the musical segment of her life which would launch her into the next phase of her career. It was a major turning point for Murray and the opportunity to give up the entertainment grind for a while and regain control over her personal activities.

For a time there would be a break from controversy over her image, an end to dealing with whom she was to the public versus whom she was to herself. It would represent a vacation from trying to deal with an over-riding will to do well in music and, at the same time, exercise the demands of her own personality. Although Murray would remain elusive in character to her public for many years to come, 1975 reflected the beginning of the days when, at the least, Murray was not elusive to herself.

And there were issues, questions, and negative components to a star's musical career that, during this hiatus, she simply would not miss. For a time, she would be removed for the most part from the ongoing battle to have good press created for her and bad press resisted by Leonard Rambeau and company.

It was a grim circumstance of foreshadowing that saw Bob Dunne open his profile of Murray in *Beetle* with the following: "Anne Murray, back home for a few days after a lengthy whirlwind tour of North America, sits in her living room talking about some letters she'd received from a disturbed young man. Her husky voice travels the length of the sprawling, gold carpeted living room. There is an undeniable look of disquiet in her eyes as she tells the story."

"He's a writer from Canada living in the Boston area now. I don't know what he's got against me but these letters started with a weird religious angle and then he got into a perverted sexual thing.

"The letters became progressively more sexual, but he always signed his name. There was no problem in tracking him down, so the local police paid him a visit or two and straightened the whole matter out."

The reference, common sometimes for musical performers who have reached the levels of stardom that Murray had attained by this time, nonetheless reflected that less wholesome aspect of entertainment fame and success. It also foreshadowed one of the more well-known cases of erotomania which would launch Murray into the news media in a different way for a number of years both nationally and internationally.

Murray, by this time, was no stranger to media questions that focused on both her own sexuality and the sexuality of her audience. And, to her credit, she had become adept by this time to responding to the questions, virtually irrelevant where music was concerned, with good humor and a serious attempt to understand. After all, hadn't a great deal been made about her apparent lesbian following? And hadn't she sighed and responded honestly to the questions? In both cases, the answer was yes.

"It was *Rolling Stone*, the U.S. music bible, that first noted her growing lesbian following," wrote George Anthony in his 1975 *Chatelaine* profile. "At one badly publicized date in Chicago 'they were the only ones who showed up, so needless to say I was awfully glad to see them.' It wasn't until she returned to Toronto for the symphony concert that she heard the story that she herself was a lesbian.

" 'Have you ever heard that story?' she asked. I said yes, sure, I'd heard it, but it was so old now, and said about everybody in the business sooner or later.

" 'Awwwww,' she said, as if I had been holding out on her. 'It's not old stuff to me! I mean, I've never heard it in Toronto before. When Dusty Springfield was singing over here she went to this gay bar in Vancouver and people there told her I was gay. 'Well, I'm not,' I told her. 'Gosh,' she said, 'they're going to be *awfully* disappointed!'" Anne and Leonard (Rambeau was apparently on hand for the interview) both cracked up."

Said Murray: "The only rough time was in Baton Rouge, Louisiana. I was there for a concert and just got into my hotel room when, uh, these two big — uh, girls — walk in with motorcycle helmets under their arms. 'We want autographs!' they said, and I said, 'Yessir!" ' (She did a mock salute.) "There was no way I was gonna argue with either one of them!"

Apparently Murray tried to analyze the attraction in the beginning. "Figured maybe it was the phys-ed thing — you know, all those stories about teaching gym in P.E.I. Then I mentioned it to Helen Reddy, and she said 'That's funny — I've got the same following and I've never taught gym in P.E.I.' When I told Peggy Lee about it she laughed. '*All* girls singers get that,' she told me. 'I've had that for *years*.' Streisand has a bigger gay following than all of us."

Larry LeBlanc's story in the 1974 *Maclean's* also tended to dismiss as typical the now seemingly endless reports of a lesbian following. "Audiences pick their stars, not the other way around, and even though Anne remains decidedly heterosexual she has the flinty good looks, the athletic figure, broad shoulders and boyish hairstyle that naturally make her a darling of the butch set. It may even be as the Chicago *Tribune* wrote: 'There's always going to be this lingering whiff of phys-ed classes about the woman.' Peggy Lee had a lesbian following. So did Janis Joplin. Why not Anne?"

Although the list of female performers with lesbian followers was getting longer, so long in fact it could cover quite literally every female performer, the topic kept coming up in the media, regardless of her marriage to Langstroth and her giving birth to two children, as writer Dennis Hunt demonstrated at the time. "Indirectly her sports association has been responsible, she speculated, for the only thing about her that's at all controversial — her large lesbian following. This is unusual, in her words, for 'a straight-laced mother of two who is happily married and not very exciting.' Murray offered reasons for attracting this bloc of gay women fans and came up with these possibilities: her athlete's build and gait, and the fact that she's an ex-physical education teacher (according to a popular stereotype, many female gym teachers are gay).

" 'Who really knows why?' she asked. 'The lesbians have been there since the beginning of my career, and they've been staunch supporters. I'm not complaining. I appreciate the support. It's just a little strange, that's all.'

"Murray is rather blase about the fact that a lot of people think she's gay. 'I hear that all the time,' she explained. 'I just laugh about it. It's neither here nor there to me. When I got married I remember getting a letter from somebody saying that it was a good cover. When I had the first child I got a letter saying that's another good cover and why don't I come out of the closet.'

"Suspecting Murray of homosexuality is ironic considering the natural limits placed on her by her profession. 'I travel in a world of men,' she pointed out. 'It's the nature of the business. I have no sisters and only a handful of women friends. I don't see much of women at all.' "

After recounting a similar story and point of view to writer Chet Flippo, she recounted yet another. "I have been mauled. I was in the washroom of a club in Atlanta and I was sitting on the can and all these honeys were looking under the partition and were after me. Really got out of hand. My stage manager had to punch one of them out. Any audience — a lot of them feel they own you and they just take strips out of you. I've never refused an autograph. I owe the audience something, but not *everything*. The more you give, the more they want and you can only give so much. I get all these labels — Canada's ambassador, Canada's sweetheart — and people ask me, 'Do you feel any responsibility?' I feel no responsibility to anyone whatsoever, to Canada or to any other place for that matter."

Murray's remarks smacked of an almost painful honesty. Earlier in the article she had been asked, yet again, about projecting the girl-next-door image, if it was really her. "Yeah, I guess it is, and that bothered me in the beginning. But I always looked healthy. I keep myself in good condition, I don't tell people to fuck off. I'm as close to the girl next door as you can get. I once did a Top Forty radio interview in L.A. and the guy asked me if *Snowbird* was a cocaine song. Now if had it to do over, I would say, '*Yes*, definitely.' "

In 1975, Murray was tired of playing the game with the media, was tired of manipulating her image and almost apologizing for approaching her career with a sense of ambition and self-direction. It was time to take some time off and live with some perspective. In a business which often survives on hype and image, Murray had decided to simply be herself. As she had told George Anthony earlier that year, "I intended to have a private life."

One of the most obvious demonstrations of that commitment to a private life came on her birthday that year, her thirtieth. This time she celebrated June 20th by marrying Bill Langstroth in a service performed at home by a priest. As far as is known, the news media was taken by surprise, not knowing about the wedding until a few days after it was over. It was also reported that her parents did not even know in advance and some of her siblings until a few days after the event had taken place. According to writer David Livingstone, the bride wore green and went shoeless. It seemed more than a wedding. It seemed an act of independence, a commitment to privacy, a moving away from all the hype and glitter which, of necessity, characterized the career side of her life.

The wedding also ended speculation in some quarters that it was Leonard Rambeau whom she would eventually marry. Although by this time, Langstroth was known to be the man in her life by some — in fact, her affair with him had been discussed as gossip for some time in the Maritimes — there were those who felt Rambeau was a possibility because of his close friendship and ever-present proximity. Murray had come out of the closet, all right, but with regard to Langstroth. The private matter that she later admitted had been festering since 1968 had finally surfaced and had been made official. The idea now was to begin her family and it would be only a few months until she was carrying their first child.

Although Murray was enjoying a hiatus from the music business, Capitol Records was continuing to release her music through a number of new recordings. These included the singles *Sunday Sunrise, The Call*, and *Uproar* in 1975, plus *Things* and *Golden Oldie* in 1976, and *Sunday School To Broadway* in 1977. As for LPs issued during this period, TOGETHER in October of 1975 and KEEPING IN TOUCH in the fall of 1976 were the offerings. Although in virtually every case the releases made the charts, none of them was a massive success.

While Murray was embarked on the private and family life she had wanted for so long, there were changes afoot in the music end as well. It was time for some departures, especially in production.

The Maritime Mafia lost its first component when one of the "Bs" in Balmur departed Toronto for Los Angeles. Brian Ahern, intent on starting his own production company there, left amicably to do so. He would not connect again with Balmur until nearly 15 years later when he would produce an album for Balmur's client, country singer George Fox. Ahern, meanwhile, would work with Emmylou Harris and even be married to her for a time. And when Ahern produced an album for Mary Kay Place, Harris and Murray would do some back-up vocals, just to help out.

Skip Beckwith, long time bassist and musical director in her band, also gave it all up, reportedly tired of both touring and Toronto. Returning to Halifax, after parting company on good terms with Murray, he built a home and returned to jazz. Eventually, he moved to Antigonish, Nova Scotia, to teach in the jazz program at Saint Francis Xavier University. Beckwith later told writers Virginia Beaton and Stephen Peterson that he had only high praise of Murray. "I stayed with her for six years and I never heard her sing one note out of tune. Ever, on any of those shows. Monitors or no monitors, she has the voice." And he would confess that his favorite Murray recording was the 1974 album, HIGHLY PRIZED POSSESSION.

For the next couple of years, Murray would focus on her private life generally and motherhood in particular, which found its focus in the birth of her first child, William Stewart Langstroth Jr. in August of 1976. A daughter, Dawn Joann, joined the family April 20, 1979. Her focus on motherhood was noted in some detail by the ever-present George Anthony in another of his pieces for *Chatelaine* late in 1976.

"I haven't worked since June. Haven't sung a note. Not one note. Haven't missed it one bit, either.

"I get up around noon or so and I spend an hour or so deciding which maternity top to wear. Then, later, I have to decide where I'm going to sit and do nothing — outside or inside, in the living room, in the rec room. Then I have to decide whether I'm going to read a book or watch TV. And sometimes I change into *another* maternity top later in the day. All day long, it's decisions, decisions, decisions!"

As Anthony reported: "Bill (Langstroth) has two grown-up

children by his first marriage, but he and Anne decided to go the whole route and attend prenatal classes. He was determined to be at her side from beginning to end, and together they learned the breathing techniques: he as coach and she as his star pupil."

Murray took *Chatelaine* readers right into the delivery room. "I was having a lot of pain, because the baby was pressing on my spine, but they were afraid to give me another spinal. I said 'Oh, that's okay, go right ahead!' — not realizing that they were afraid I'd get too relaxed to push. Finally I caught on, but by this time everything was getting very hazy. I was quite indignant about the whole thing. *I'll show them a thing or two,* I thought. *They don't know what great shape I'm in. They don't know I used to be a phys-ed teacher. They don't know I can still swim 30 lengths in the pool, I'll show them.*

"And all the time I was thinking this, I actually thought I was saying it. Thought I was telling them all where to get off. Bill was right there, of course. Says I didn't say a word. Not a single word. Just looked stunned through the whole thing. But when they said push, I *pushed*. And out he came. I could hear Bill saying, 'There's his head!' And my doctor, who's so quiet as a rule, suddenly cried, 'It's a *boy*!' and I remember looking around and thinking, 'Who said *that*?' It was over that fast. At one point I looked up and there was this doctor I hadn't seen before, in a green cap and gown and surgical mask, holding *my* baby. I thought, *now who the hell is that*? It was Bill. I'd forgotten he'd scrubbed up with the rest of them. When I saw the baby's black hair I was amazed. I thought, *how could I have a baby with black hair*? Then I remembered. *Oh yeah — Bill!*"

Anthony also reported that Murray, asked by a nurse how the experience was, replied, "Better than a hit record."

Ultimately, Murray would maintain that her children were the most important component of her life. "As much as I sometimes might want to try other things, my children are more important to me than everything," she told Lee Anne Nicholson of *TV Guide* more than a decade later. And earlier than that, she told *US Magazine*: "As soon as I built my career around my family life, everything — the career and my own feelings about myself — improved." And she meant what she said. Even when she returned to work as a singer and her career blossomed yet again, she divided her time between work, a private life in Toronto with regular visits to Nova Scotia, and an attention to children generally which would include work as chair of the Canada Save the Children Fund, work for which she would receive tribute in Canada, especially for adopting three foster children as part of her contribution to the program. There were even benefit concerts to raise money for the Fund. Murray planned her schedule around her private life and then permitted only those concert or television engagements which fitted into that schedule.

On the heels of the birth of her son, Murray also recorded a children's album, THERE'S A HIPPO IN MY TUB, in 1977, serving as associate producer on the project. Released on Capitol Records in Canada, it was released by Sesame Street Records in the United States.

It was this requirement for family life which apparently inspired an apparent about face in another area. When Murray agreed to be the commercial spokesperson for the Canadian Imperial Bank of Commerce (CIBC), critics complained that she had turned establishment. Going back, some of them had reason to be confused. Murray had once appeared quite critical of Canadian skier Nancy Greene in the media for her promotion of Mars bars. Nonetheless, Murray was intent now on concentrating on her marriage and family, and the CIBC contract seemed a means of satisfying that requirement. At a press conference in Halifax in 1977, she admitted the money from the arrangement would permit more time with her children and less time on the road.

Nor was she going to forget her roots in Springhill either. It was during this period that she returned to her hometown to participate in her high school reunion, an event reported in some detail by The Springhill-Parrsboro *Record* in its July 27, 1978 edition, complete with a photograph of The Freshettes (Murray, Geraldine Hopkins, and Cathy Ross), reunited for the occasion. In the photograph, Murray holds a ukulele.

"Over 2,000 packed the Springhill Arena on Thursday night, July 20, when the students of the classes of 1957-1964 presented one of the best, most professional-like concerts ever seen in Springhill. The highlight of the evening was Anne Murray, who, being home for the reunion, took part in the show and delighted the audience with her singing and her easy-going manner which created instant rapport.

"The show, from beginning to end, was nothing less than terrific, sending everyone away after two hours still wishing for more. The response from the enthusiastic audience built to such a pitch that the entertainers gave everything they had to their individual numbers.

"Amiable Rud Osmond emceed the program and entertained the crowd with his wit."

The coverage of the event gives a detailed rundown of all the performers. Murray performed *In My Father's House* with The Freshettes, accompanying them on the ukulele, and she performed *You Needed Me*, accompanied by Stewart Murray and Lamont King. "Anne told the audience she had just released her 15th album, which meant she had recorded approximately 150 songs. She then delighted the audience with a song from her children's album, *Hey, Daddy There's A Dragon In The Driveway* (later she had the audience sing along with her). The audience accorded her a standing ovation."

Murray also took part in a "Girl's Choral Group" and led the finale to the evening. And Bill Langstroth was busy throughout the evening as well. He and Murray's brother, Stewart, accompanied a Men's Choral Group and soloist Geraldine Hopkins.

Murray would later call this period of her life a period of semi-retirement, although it was far from inactive. There continued to be records, television specials, and some concerts, a tour of Japan and even some participation in sporting events. Rather than a period of semi-retirement, it was a regrouping.

In another sense, the enigma of just who Anne Murray was, to the public who watched her every move, was now intensifying. Her evolution from reluctant singer to *Snowbird* star to girl-next-door to ambitious performer with a focus on image, to married woman and mother with a passion for her private life, to hometown girl at her high school reunion would continue. In 1978 she was on the brink, not only of continued stardom, but *super*stardom.

Although the people of Springhill could not know it at the

time, Murray's performance of *You Needed Me* at her high school reunion was an ironic link with what would greet visitors to the Anne Murray Centre there more than a decade later. In the museum dedicated to her achievements, a recording of her voice would explain that *You Needed Me* was her favorite song, a song which came along to re-ignite her career. And it would bring her even more accolades and honors as a reigning pop music star.

Even more importantly, she would be able to approach her career and her life on her own terms. THIS WAY IS MY WAY, the title of her first Capitol Records LP, would become more than just a title. Still, there would be something rather elusive about Morna Anne Murray in the hearts of her Canadian fans.

Anne with her son, William Langstroth Jr.

ANNE
MURRAY
HIGHLY
PRIZED
POSSESSION

Bill Langstroth took the photos for both the front and back covers of LET'S KEEP IT THAT WAY *featuring* You Needed Me, *the song which made her a superstar.*

CHAPTER SEVEN

Let's Keep It That Way

You know how people go off the deep end with this success thing; they overdo it and before you know it, they're buried, because people are sick of hearing about them, sick of seeing them. I wanted to do this thing deliberately, slowly. I wanted to move it so that it would last for some time — so that when these kids grow up, I'll still have a career.

— Anne Murray

By 1978, happily embarked on the life of marriage and mother-hood she had sought for so long, and, as she had proclaimed herself many times, finally having found a balance between career and her powerful need for a private life, Anne Murray, still a musical star, was perhaps unaware that she was poised on the last incline before superstardom. The LP was LET'S KEEP IT THAT WAY. The song was *You Needed Me*, the tune she would describe well into the 1990s as still her favorite.

Much has been made of the song itself, how *You Needed Me* so perfectly suited her voice, how its warm sentiments and pretty melody were a perfect vehicle for the rich way in which Murray would interpret the lyrics. But the song was more than that. In truth it represented a musical signpost in Murray's previously ambivalent approach to her life and the music in it. It served to testify musically to the place in her life at which she'd now arrived, in control of her own career rather than her career in con-trol of *her*, married and raising a family, no longer suffering the whims of or concerns about musical categorization, which tours to take, which clubs to endure. No gala openings in Los Angeles would be required now, nor would she have to jam long tours into her life to keep her star shining. Not only because she was about to achieve the level of success where she could set her own terms, but because her own terms had already been set — on the level which mattered most, her own personal definition of self, goals, and direction.

The album cover of LET'S KEEP IT THAT WAY depicts the relative peace and tranquility which Murray had somehow finally achieved in her life. Gone were questions of all or nothing with respect to her career, considerations about image makeover, anxiety about how to pursue her career and still maintain her sense of self. The front and back LP cover photos of Murray, both taken by her hus-band, Bill Langstroth, demonstrate the essential control which had entered her life by this time. The natural smile and straight-into-the-camera gaze on the cover of the LP seems to show a Murray who knows exactly where she is going and where she intends never to return. The image captures the amalgam of char-acteristics she had become. Perhaps there remains a glimpse of the woman-next-door, but the spirited Murray with opinions to match is there. The photograph is so natural, one cannot help but see the balance which has been apparently achieved. Yes, she is ambitious, yet the photograph conveys a kind of post-achievement calm. The back cover photograph captures the same mood in a broader sense. Calm waters stretching towards a nearly limitless horizon, Murray strolling pensively, her back to the camera, along a stone-littered beach, as if she now has the time to enjoy having arrived. And tucked into the left hand corner of this photograph is the dedication, "This Album is for Bill — love Anne."

A clip at the Anne Murray Centre in Springhill describes her personal preference for the song *You Needed Me*, mentions briefly how it came along at the right time in her career. It's possible Murray means in the clip that she was due for another hit record, but this is doubtful in view of her personal achievements during the same period. More likely, it came along at the right time as musical endorsement of the point of calm resolve she had reached in her personal life. And in spite of the fact Murray did not author the song, the tune was instead composed by Randy Goodrum, her interpretation of it is so powerful it became a kind of authorship. Indeed, as she transforms the lyrics into her own, they seem afterwards addressed to Langstroth, or at least to Langstroth, their children, and that component of her life which had at long last permitted her to address her own priorities:

> *I cried a tear*
> *You wiped it dry*
> *I was confused*
> *You cleared my mind*
> *I sold my soul*
> *You bought it back for me*
> *And held me up and gave me dignity*
> *Somehow you needed me.*

As an album, LET'S KEEP IT THAT WAY also reflected a blend of old and new. Produced by Jim Ed Norman, who had worked with The Eagles, a producer willing, as Murray stated, to come to Toronto and live in a hotel alone for months until the project was complete, in contrast to predecessor Tom Catalano who wanted her to telephone her vocals to Los Angeles. Norman offered a fresh approach, yet on *You Needed Me* the strings were arranged by Rick Wilkins whose string arrangements nearly a decade before on *Snowbird* had, for many, made all the difference on her first hit record. The album included a version of the traditional *Tennessee Waltz* but also contemporary numbers composed by Kim Carnes and Kenny Rogers.

From the standpoint of music alone, the album was a triumph over such efforts as TOGETHER and KEEPING IN TOUCH. After working with Brian Ahern for ten albums, Tom Catalano had been chosen by Capitol Records as her producer in the wake of Ahern's departure. Somehow, however, there was a change of attitude which Murray realized accompanied the production change. While under Catalano's production, Murray was pressured into recording material she did not like. KEEPING IN TOUCH is her least favorite album. TOGETHER wasn't much better, although Murray did profoundly enjoy working with Dusty Springfield and Dianne Brooks who performed back-up vocal chores. (In the liner notes of the LP *Danny's Song*, Murray says: "This album is dedicated to Dianne Gwendolyn Brooks who has been a constant source of inspiration.") The resounding success of LET'S KEEP IT THAT WAY and *You Needed Me* not only accelerated her musical career even further, but endorsed her production and management choices, rising above the methods of managers like Shep Gordon and even the demands of Capitol Records.

Norman had first met Murray in 1976 when she was doing a television show in Los Angeles. "I was over in London, conducting strings for the Eagles when I first met Leonard Rambeau. Leonard wanted us to get together the next time Anne came to L.A. I didn't know her albums because I've never been much of an album person. But I knew her singles, especially some of the country singles that hadn't been pop hits. Like that Kenny Rogers song she did so well, *Stranger In My Place*."

As it turned out, Norman dropped by her dressing room a few months later while Murray was in Hollywood doing a Seals and Croft special. "We asked her all the usual things — where she wanted to go from here, what direction she was looking for, that sort of thing. She spent most of the time sizing me up. I told her that I thought the albums she had done with Tom Catalano were, for me, off the mark. But if she wanted to get back to where she'd been, and start making some hit singles again, I was interested." Murray was interested too.

"I think she's a phenomenal singer," Norman has said, "but so are some other female singers. The thing that distinguishes her is her ease; she sounds very comfortable when she sings. She's the most effortless singer I know — which may be why she's always able to communicate the lyric of the song as well as the melody. In any case, we make beautiful music together." Murray would complain many times that her voice conveys an ease which denies the effort she put into singing songs. She said it was inaccurate to assume because her singing sounded easy that she did not have to work hard to sing.

"Her family life was apparently something she considered inviolate, a world to be guarded jealously — but something about the timing of it was obviously propitious," wrote Jay Teitel in a May 1980 *Chatelaine* article. "During the same span that she had begun 'nesting', she had also come up with a new manager, Leonard Rambeau . . . , a new producer, Jim Ed Norman (of Eagles fame), and a new song, Randy Goodrum's *You Needed Me* (the one with the pedestal in it). She was also being touted in *Variety*, along with Linda Ronstadt, as the most dependable pop recording artist in the industry."

Noting, as had others, that Murray was the favorite artist (female) of Elvis Presley, Teitel's *Chatelaine* article reports that Murray did not hesitate to suggest that *control* was the reason for the turn of events in her career during the post *You Needed Me* period.

" 'Control,' she says with no hesitation. 'I know what I'm doing today where I never did before. I've got a plan.' " Murray went on to say: "When I had that conversation in '75 with my manager, Shep Gordon, and I said, 'I've got to stop now,' the reason was all control, a complete lack of it, that is. There was no strategy being laid out, no plan of attack. It was a mishmash . . . Part of it was me, I'm sure. Maybe I wasn't totally committed before; I don't think I was. Every time I'd get close to being pushed over the top, that intangible top, I'd back off. Maybe I was scared, I don't know."

Teitel suggested that she might not feel she deserved it, referring, he wrote, to the Canadian inferiority complex. But Murray was adamant that such was not the case. "Uh-uh. Someone asked me the other day whether I felt guilty about going to Vegas, making all that money. I don't feel guilty about it at all. I've paid my dues. And people pay to see me. No, I think it was more a fear of change. I was afraid, if I became a success, I'd get glassy-eyed — you know, where the wall goes up and you don't look people in the eye? I've seen that happen to people in this business — really, they just don't see you anymore. If can be really insulting if you're not aware of it."

But Murray was able to see the relationship clearly between the demands of her career and family and derived a satisfaction from having her life organized, complete with a sure knowledge that it was give and take, that there would be sacrifices. There seemed to be rewards in being in control of her life, rewards which emerged from surprising quarters. It was as if fate was endorsing all her choices.

"In the fall of '77," she said, "Leonard called me up from L.A. one day, my agent was on another line, a conference call, and Leonard said, 'Get our your calendar, we're going to plan 1978.' And in an hour and a half we had the year planned. That had never happened before. And then things just started to fall into place. I had a new house, and a new baby, and of course a new hit song, *You Needed Me*, which might have been the luckiest thing of all because someone had enough faith to send it to me when I was stone cold. I mean I couldn't have been colder . . . I was *ready* for children. I was 30 years old. Children are amazing, aren't they? . . . They're also a pain in the ass, mind you. This last one, Dawn, the baby, she was eating every two hours, and she had night and day mixed up on top of it. At 3 a.m., she was just getting ready to boogie. But it's a sacrifice you make gladly, don't you?"

In the aftermath of the phenomenal success of *You Needed Me*, Murray would be vaulted into the status of true superstar, would take home a pop Grammy, and would forever be able to set her own professional terms, playing sold-out shows at the Royal Alexandra Theatre in Toronto and Radio City Music Hall and

Carnegie Hall in New York, instead of clubs where even a visit to the bathroom might be a relatively dangerous proposition.

As Murray's first decade as a star in the music business was coming to a close, the ambivalence that had characterized the period until her marriage to Langstroth and the birth of their first child now seemed to be clearly over. Murray had said many times that achieving her ambition to start a family would serve to clear up her personal questions surrounding her career. She claimed that having a child would convince her that she was capable of anything and, being capable of anything, she would pursue her musical career with renewed vigor. This attitude was clear in an article which appeared in *The Toronto Sun* in 1978. As she told journalist Joan Sutton, she had toyed frequently with the idea of retiring from the music business during the 1970s.

"There have been many times in the past when the number of people on the payroll bothered me. . . . "When I was on the road, playing to half houses, I'd think 'Why don't I just quit?' But I don't think I'll ever quit and I didn't think I'd ever say that."

Sutton's reminder that Murray had once claimed the opposite, that once she had a family she would retire, gave Murray pause to consider the various points of view she had maintained in interviews, "statements that now haunt her."

"I've had my wrists slapped about the Bank of Commerce commercials because I once said I'd never do commercials. But when I decided that I wanted to be home more because of William we had to find ways to make that possible. People think I should be able to live off my income and I could, but there's no way that I could generate the money we need to maintain our overhead out of income. I have to have an office, and I have to have a band — there are 15 people permanently in my employ.

"Priorities change in life and people just have to make allowances for that. I can't believe I said all those things, but the trouble is they're there in print or on tape. Other people say all kinds of things but nobody hears them. I was naive. I was picked up out of Nova Scotia Godalmighty, and dropped in Hollywood. I'd like to see how most people could handle that, even to be picked up in Toronto and dropped in Hollywood — it's a shock."

George Anthony wrote a similar sentiment in a promotional

piece on Murray. "I was plucked out of Springhill, Nova Scotia and dropped on a Hollywood soundstage. I felt like Dorothy in Oz. Exactly like Dorothy, come to think of it. All I wanted to do was go home."

"I certainly don't believe in doing commercials," Murray told Paul King in *Today*. "I think it's unfair for performers to use their influence over people." King admitted that she had apparently changed her tune. "I've been with the Commerce since my first bank account and I'm as proud of those commercials as anything I've done."

Later, Murray amplified on her new approach to commercial sponsorship in an interview with Perry Stern. "I don't think a person out in the audience gives a shit whether I'm being sponsored by Ford. Do you think they hear *You Needed Me* and think about Ford. Give me a break. Maybe there's some subliminal thing when they walk through the lobby and they see a car that might suggest to them some other time that they might buy an Escort. I don't know, that doesn't concern me at all."

By the time *You Needed Me* had vaulted Murray into superstardom, however, it was apparent that she was ready for the position, due mainly to being fulfilled as a wife and mother.

"All of a sudden, after I gave birth to my first child, I had a focus, a reason. Maybe I didn't think I was important enough to be successful before that," she told writer Micki Moore. "I always wanted to have children and I always thought that was one of my purposes in life, and once I started having them, I just felt like I could take on anything. I felt that anything I decided to try, I could do. Whether that was because I didn't have my first child until I was 31 . . . maybe I was just getting nervous and feeling like I was running out of time. I don't know if all those 'mother' things are true, about being fulfilled and all of that you read about, but I certainly felt all those things."

It was also now apparent that, child and family in hand, Murray was clearly calling the shots. Moore suggested a more accurate description of the apple-cheeked girl-next-door might be "a consummate, dynamic businesswoman."

"Yes, that's a better picture of me and people don't know that. It started after I had my son William with this renewed confidence and direction. I sat down with all the people in my career, and Leonard Rambeau decided he could take over my management. I had new record producers and I said, 'We're going to plan this. These are the rules: I have a child now, the career has to work around the family.' "

Murray frankly admitted that, on occasion, there were difficulties in booking a "mother" instead of "an aggressive starlet."

"Exactly. And he [Rambeau] has trouble with that a lot of times. You see, at that time I was dealing with men. They had been married, but none had children. They couldn't understand that I had this album and I could not just go for broke and go after it. You can't do that. You've got a baby, you've got responsibility. Besides, I needed something as an excuse to do this thing sanely. You know how people go off the deep end with this success thing; they overdo it and before you know it, they're buried, because people are sick of hearing about them, sick of seeing them. I wanted to do this thing deliberately, slowly. I wanted to move it so that it would last for some time — so that when those kids grow up, I'll still have a career. I didn't want to jump into it. I wanted to make them part of my life. I realized very early that if you're going to have a career, you're going to have to do it with children and it's all going to have to happen at once. You don't go and have your babies, then do your career. That's not enjoying your life — working and not doing anything else, shutting out tennis and golf, and all those other things. It all happens at once and you can make it happen right."

Attributing her ability to know what she needs and wants with learning to handle strong men while growing up with five brothers, she added, "I'm also very open to advice. I'll listen till the cows come home to everybody. I had these people around me. They would advise me, and I would say, 'This is what I think,' they would say, 'This is what we think,' and I'd say, 'Okay, this is what's going to happen.' "

Part of the reason Murray could decide to pursue her career aggressively, of course, was an acceptance on Bill Langstroth's part that she would be the career breadwinner.

"Yes, I think so," Murray told Moore. "We knew that right from the beginning. We talked about it and he understood that. So, when I'm away, he just takes over and when I'm at home, I take over. The two of us are involved in everything. I know he's there with the kids and he's a great father, so I can leave and know everything's going to be looked after. It's not the same as leaving them with a housekeeper. And even though he comes from a television background, we made a conscious decision that he would not participate in my career. I just didn't think it worked. I wanted the two things separate. He had no problem with that."

By the end of the decade the great success of *You Needed Me* had endorsed Murray's newfound focus on control, of her life and her career. Apparent reversals of image, opinion, and even her career priorities showed only that she had decided she had a clear view of where she was going, not only as a musical superstar, but as a woman, mother, and spouse. While her success reversed her opinions about such issues as performing in Las Vegas or whether to endorse the CIBC in commercials, there were other issues about which she remained adamant. For example, she would continue to record in Toronto.

As George Anthony reported in a special advertising supplement to *Billboard* in October, 1979, the mellowing of Anne Murray provided "maybes" where once the answer had been "nos."

"Not that she's eliminated the word no from her professional vocabulary," he said. "She still refused to move to California, making her home in Toronto instead. And she still insists on recording her albums there, much to the chagrin of West Coast nay-sayers, who still believe Rodeo Drive is the centre of the universe. But Anne Murray had the last laugh when the Rolling Stones and other discerning disk-cutters started to flock to that Canadian city to wax their songs. And if *Billboard* chart records are any indication, she hasn't suffered."

Indeed, Murray was not suffering. In 1978 she received three Grammy nominations, including Best Pop Vocal Performer, Female; Record of the Year; and Best Country Vocal Performer, Female. Her competition that year in the pop female performer category was fierce, namely Carly Simon, Donna Summer, Olivia Newton John, and Barbra Streisand. But after the smoke had cleared, while Murray watched with her family from her home, she had won the Grammy. Coupled with the emblazoning of her name in Nashville's Music

Hall of Fame and song of the year at the Academy of Country Music Awards for *You Needed Me*, Murray was most definitely in a position to call her own tune. Which was exactly what she did.

Over the years, Murray had expressed her reservations about performing in the glitter capitol, Las Vegas. For one thing, in the early days of her performances there, she had run awry of the management by sporting bare feet and hot pants, then the fashion rage, and had been asked to change her clothes. Murray was adamant that she did not like hotels. Nick Sevano consistently wanted to book her into Las Vegas while she wanted to tour the college circuit. The result was Murray's boycott of Vegas performances until late in the decade when, armed with a powerful contract, with accommodation made for her family, she could return in triumph, all her conditions met for performance.

Murray did her part as well. If Vegas was prepared to pay her a fortune to perform, to meet all her requirements, she would appear there like the superstar she was, with a visually overhauled image of new hairdo and sequined gowns. And by this time, the performer was a consummate professional, able to disarm her audience with between-song banter which included her passion for Canada's favorite sport. Often she mentioned having to phone out for the hockey scores. There were even reports of her addition of a soft shoe routine to the act.

As George Anthony reported, "Hotels don't hate her, especially in Vegas. She said no to that town too (while her managers gnashed their teeth) for six years until the Aladdin coaxed her back. Now she has a megabuck deal with the Riviera for six weeks work. Included in the deal are a dozen rooms for her musicians and staff plus a three-bedroom home, fully staffed, for the lady who hates hotels." Added Anthony: "The girl who once complained she didn't like 'being served up like dessert' to nightclub audiences in gambling spas has a Cherries Jubilee price tag now. Not that she's suffered financially up to now. Her annual income passed the $1 million mark some time ago, without Vegas paychecks."

Ironically, however, it was seeing her name in lights in the desert city which finally drove home the message that she was a star. "I looked out the window one day and there was Frank

Sinatra's marquee across the street and there was mine. I thought: Anne, you really are in show business now," she told writer Perry Stern in *Canadian Musician*.

And certainly, according to Paul King, the show in Vegas was a success. With comedian Rodney Dangerfield opening for her, the emcee introducing her often was drowned out by a rising crescendo in the room.

"You don't hear the rest," reported King. "The house has exploded in a thunderous ovation. The people know whom they've come to hear. After all, her face smiles out from nine huge billboards on the Strip and from posters at every bus-stop bench. And her name stands yards high on that massive sign out front — larger than Tom Jones's or Mac Davis's down the street, and a storey above Dangerfield's (said Rodney when asked if he knew her, 'Sure, But does *she* know me?') In Las Vegas, mecca of big-name acts, Anne Murray is suddenly superstar.

"The curtains open on her own 10-piece band, singers Debbie Schaal and kid-brother Bruce Murray, plus an 18-member house orchestra in black tie — all surrounded by potted palms bathed in midnight blue light. And then Anne Murray strides on like a former phys-ed teacher, in a floor-length, metallic blue gown.

"Cheeks like apples, blonde hair feathering her forehead, she flashes white-toothed acknowledgement to the cheering crowd and instantly seduces it with a husky *Why Don't You Stick Around*. The applause increases as the hit songs follow. *Snowbird, Danny's Song, Daydream Believer, Broken Hearted Me, Shadows in the Moonlight, You Needed Me*. In between comes the wry, homespun patter that sounds spontaneous but is as carefully calculated as her lip syncing on most TV talk shows.

" 'Take off your tie or girdle,' she grins, 'and put your feet up on the people in front of you.' She dons a top hat, snaps a shoulder, swishes across the stage. 'See?' she laughs. 'You can dress her up but . . .' They love it.

"When she asks, 'Any Canadians here?' and gets some yells, she banters, 'Hey, you're well behaved.' Then she adds, 'But I'm always disappointed that you're put in the back.'

" 'No more,' someone shouts, and the crowd erupts. Anne beams. It's pure romance, Nova Scotia wooing Middle America."

King reported that there was an honesty about Murray's performance at the root of the cheers and ovations from the audience members. "They know what they're doing. They're responding not only to a sensational voice but to that stage rarity: sincerity. Murray's naturalness transposes into enormous charm, particularly for those who are sick of showbiz gimmicks and glitter. She is simply one of them; or perhaps, in essence, what they would like to be. When producers once told her to 'get with it, show more boob, use a few four-letter words,' she answered, 'The hell with you. All I've got is my voice. I won't change a thing.' "

When she performed in the main room at the Riviera — two shows nightly, every one a sellout, "twenty-eight shows, twenty-eight hours, twenty-eight numbers a night" — she collected $500,000, and when she was asked back for six weeks the following year, the new contract was $1 million.

Amid all this success, however, Murray the family woman was still in evidence. King reported that not far away from the Riviera performance, her children, their nanny, and her husband were in residence in a million-dollar ranch house — complete with tennis courts, pool, chauffeured Rolls, and armed guard — that the Riviera had provided. There was that sense of control and balance. Murray had not given up music when she began her family and, as she told King, she was glad she hadn't. At last, she had been able to achieve what she wanted, her family and success in music, both perfectly coordinated on her terms to permit them to co-exist.

"Now, if I'd quit I'd be bored. I love to sing, but not necessarily to crowds. The adulation I can do entirely without. I never wanted it. But the rest is a challenge. I said to myself, dammit, I can do it. And right now I just want it all to keep going this way. I hope it lasts for another twenty years."

A report from Vegas for the Toronto news media by George Anthony implied Murray seemed to even enjoy the notoriety of her response there. "At night she made her first appearance in public, attending Kenny Rogers' closing night at the Riviera," he wrote. "Looking elegantly chic in a new design by Juul Haalmeyer she sipped a Diet Pepsi as Rogers and Melissa Manchester performed. When Rogers told the packed showroom she was in the audience and then introduced her, shrieks of approval came with the thunderous applause, to the point that a hotel representative advised her to leave before the lights came on and arranged for her chauffeur-driven Rolls-Royce to wait at the back door so she wouldn't have to walk through the casino.

"Near the end of Rogers' show, Vegas headliners Wayne Newton and Pia Zadora made a surprise appearance on stage, presenting Rogers with a token of the hotel's appreciation — a gleaming white Stutz-Bearcat, created in Italy specially for the bearded country singer. When Ms. Murray saw that car her eyes sparkled.

" 'Fred,' she whispered, nudging her U.S. manager with a wicked gleam in her eye. 'I want one.'

"Springhill was never like this."

By the end of the 1970s, Las Vegas wasn't the only entertainment capitol Anne Murray had conquered. By then, she had sold out her concert at Carnegie Hall, as well as concerts at Radio City Music Hall and in Toronto. She was scheduled to appear with the Muppets, to satisfy her ambition to sing a duet with Miss Piggy, and was known worldwide for her concerts and various other television specials.

Toronto Star writer Peter Goddard was in New York for the Carnegie Hall performance. "It brought a touch of class," he wrote. "Down-home class that is. You can put Anne Murray in Carnegie Hall but you can't take her completely out of Springhill, N.S., where she was born.

"Plants decorated the stage. Very classy. The 13-piece New York string section behind her was tuxedoed and elegant. But the singer, in mauve pants outfit for the first half and in black for the second, seemed quite intent to let the corn grow a little high.

" 'Does this mean I have made it?' she asked at one point, the sly smile on her face. 'Oh yeah,' shouted back someone in the audience. 'Well then,' she said, 'put your feet up on the person in front of you and relax.' "

Perhaps at the apex of her career, Murray told Goddard that the changes in her fortunes even included her band. "But I like doing one-nighters now. And the reason is simple. When I turn around to look at the band (Pat Riccio, piano; George Hebert, guitar; Aiden Mason, guitar; Peter Cardinali, bass; drummer John Anderson, and steel-guitar player Brian Gatto) I see eyes staring back at me. Before I was always apprehensive about going on stage. When I would look around I'd see a bunch of junkies and alcoholics. But the band I have now really wants to play. Before, all my bands wanted to do was to get to the nearest bar."

Murray would later confess to a brief association with drugs that would end in 1971, telling Perry Stern in *Canadian Musician* that she had experimented with marijuana. She placed the publicity gimmick at the Troubador with John Lennon and company in this context. "It was very bizarre," said Murray. "It was a big Thanksgiving drunk and that was part of the gimmick. They were trying to make me part of a very hip clique of performers and that's the kind of thing that does that. Well, it goes against my very grain to do that kind of thing. It's surprising what that can do for a publicity person, and I realize that, but it bugs my ass that by being in a picture like that, all of a sudden you're hip.

"Well, I was every bit as hip as those people. The only difference between me and them was I wasn't on drugs."

Stern reported that she had dabbled in drugs with the rest of her generation. " 'I tried marijuana early on,' she shrugs, paying no mind to the illusion she's shattering. 'The first year I came to Toronto there was marijuana, hashish, and stuff and I did occasionally use it, but I didn't like where it put me. It put me on the outside lookin' in and I don't like that, so I haven't touched it since 1971.' "

In virtually every way, Murray was now in control of her life. With nearly two dozen television specials behind her at that time, her popularity ensured in dozens of countries throughout the world, she was even able to turn down movie proposals. "When Dino de Laurentis saw her picture in *Variety* he called to see if she would consider playing the lead in *Hurricane*. She thought the whole thing was a lark," crowed George Anthony, "and explained she was already booked solid for a year. Mia Farrow ended up with the role and *Hurricane* ended up as one of the major disasters of that year.

" 'But who can tell?' Murray shrugged in response. 'I've turned down some songs that have been hits for other people — *Killing*

Me Softly, I Honestly Love You — because I didn't know if they'd be hits for me. It's a very subjective thing. . . .Years ago, I learned you have to please yourself before you can please other people. And I learned the hard way.' "

And while she was pleasing herself, she was also pleasing her fans worldwide. Her chart hits of 1979 were the singles *I Just Fall in Love Again, Shadows In The Moonlight,* and *Broken-Hearted Me,* which reached number one on the country charts in December. Her album NEW KIND OF FEELING won a gold record by the end of the year as well.

And 1980 would see her frantic pace of success continue with *Daydream Believer* on the charts as well as top ranked singles like *Lucky Me, I'm Happy Just to Dance With You,* and *Could I Have This Dance,* a number one hit on the country charts in November 1980. ANNE MURRAY'S GREATEST HITS would remain in the top five into 1981 and would have, by then, accounted for three million in sales, exceeding platinum-record levels. Other charted albums in 1980 would include I'LL ALWAYS LOVE YOU and A COUNTRY COLLECTION.

In just about every way, Anne Murray was at the top of her game. But there would be continuing conflicts. Having learned to please herself, to exercise the control over her life and career that she had so deeply needed, there were other issues which would reveal that not everything develops exclusively within a performer's sense of control.

ANNE, THE WORLD IS YOUR AUDIENCE.
CONGRATULATIONS ON YOUR CONTINUED SUCCESS AS A TRULY INTERNATIONAL ARTIST.

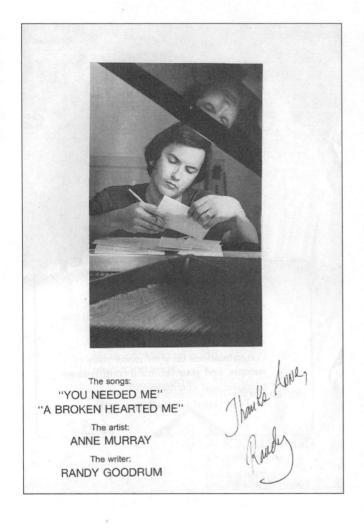

The songs:
"YOU NEEDED ME"
"A BROKEN HEARTED ME"

The artist:
ANNE MURRAY

The writer:
RANDY GOODRUM

Thanks Anne,
Randy

The world knows you
as a great singer.
I'm fortunate to know you
as a great woman.

Leonard

Prince Edward Lounge

What makes Anne
so special to us,
Is that she knows
where her roots are
And always will.
We are proud to be
one of the first places
that Anne has ever
performed and has
never forgotten.

Prince Edward Lounge
22 Weymouth Street
Charlottetown, Prince Edward Island
Canada

...AFTER 4 TELEVISION SPECIALS,
YOU'RE GETTING SO GOOD YOU SHOULD DO FIVE!

ANNE

ALAN   JOHN   DAVID

'76 "KEEPING IN TOUCH"
. . . (a cute show)

'77 "NUMBER ONE
WITH A BULLET"
. . . (cuter still)

'78 "LADIES' NIGHT"
. . . first CBC variety special sold to
U.S. commercial TV
. . . ACTRA nominee: "Best Variety
Special of the Year"
. . . highest rated CBC special of '78

'79 "ANNE MURRAY
IN JAMAICA"
. . . highest rated variety special in
Canadian television history!!!

HOLY HOCKEY PUCKS!!

You're a very nice person and we care
for you deeply . . .

ALAN THICKE—Producer/Writer

JOHN LABOE & DAVID COOK—Associate Producers

P.S. We're charging this ad to your next special.

Capitol Records inserted a feature on Anne Murray into Billboard *magazine*
which included many tributes to her from friends and colleagues.

CHAPTER EIGHT

Highly Prized Possession

A lot of Canadians don't think of me in the same terms as Linda Ronstadt, Barbra Streisand or Olivia Newton John because I'm Canadian. They take you for granted. — Anne Murray

These days, Springhill, Nova Scotia has gotten used to the fame which Anne Murray brings to it. It is, after all, for the most part, a positive kind of notoriety. If it wasn't positive, it is doubtful pedestrians would walk by the Anne Murray Centre on Main Street with scarcely a look; it is doubtful they would glance over at the building from the side door of Tim Horton's without feeling a twinge of annoyance. Springhill is still, in spite of Anne Murray, just a small town like dozens of others sprinkled across Canada like dust on a giant carpet. Small towns have a tendency to accept most things the way they are, in the way they have taken place and faded into the past, with a philosophical shrug of the shoulders.

Besides, Springhill is a community which exudes a little more warmth than most. Life goes on and you're welcome to join in. This seems to be the prevalent attitude. The unofficial breakfast club at the restaurant underneath the rooms at the Rollways Motel, for instance, seems to demonstrate that Springhill is the way Springhill has always been. There isn't any wait staff per se to refill your coffee cup. Instead, as each customer comes in — and he conveys right away that he's been coming in for years — he goes over to the coffeepot, grabs a mug and a spoon, and pours his own coffee. Then, as he's done for many a morning, he turns and asks the room at large if anyone wants a refill. Each customer does so, each in his turn. That way, the coffee mug is never empty and something hospitable has taken place too. It leaves one feeling a little like a novice in an order or a new member of an exclusive fraternity.

And it *is* a club. Everyone knows everyone else here. The conversation runs the gamut, from gun control legislation and horse racing to taxes and the rotten economy. Not that there isn't some banter. But Anne Murray doesn't come up in conversation generally, not even if there's someone staying in town doing his research and asking a question or two.

You can forget that Anne Murray attended her high school reunion here in 1978 just an instant before her stardom became superstardom. You can forget that piece of entertainment history the way you can forget that mines have exploded and caved in and that fires have burned unchecked. And you can forget that even the positive notoriety of having Anne Murray come from your town can be marred by something mysterious and misunderstood in the nature of a Saskatchewan farmer from an even smaller place than Springhill, a man who reflects a condition which has made him famous and which no one truly understands.

It's something to think about on the streets of Springhill after dark. Because it's quiet. One hardly has to look in either direction for an approaching car before crossing the street. And it's so peaceful at Tim Horton's you can hear the sound of your first sip of coffee. Which is when you think about Robert Charles Kieling and how Springhill must feel about him. Annoyance, even anger, impatience, confusion, perhaps even an unuttered sympathy. Because Kieling, certainly Canada's most famous sufferer of the condition called erotic paranoia or erotomania, has been to Springhill.

In pursuit of Anne Murray. Because he believes Anne Murray loves him and is forced, in her state of fame, to keep that love a secret.

Despite the brilliant and festive lights emanating from the Anne Murray Centre, despite Springhill's attempt to honor its famous daughter and, at the same time, derive some needed tourist dollars from her achievements, the Saskatchewan farmer has come to Springhill and, in his coming, presented for all of the town to see the more problematic other side of fame and riches. Something Anne Murray has known for a long time now. Something Springhill has learned a little more grudgingly.

In the end, Springhill probably just feels confusion. Too much *real* tragedy in its past to summon up anger over a man with a condition modern medical science isn't sure how to treat. Because, Anne Murray Centre or not, Springhill has perspective. Which is why it endures all the life it does with a kind of shrug and offhand remark.

But there is this other Anne Murray story . . .

Unaware of how wide Murray's fame has spread, many of her fans are shocked when they stumble onto it outside of

Canada," wrote Winnipeg music journalist Stephen Ostick a few years ago.

"People say to me, 'You know, I was down in Florida and they play you in the States!,' " said Murray then. "I say, 'Oh, do they?' Well, no kidding. Where do I do all my touring other than in the States? It's so funny that they say, 'Well, yeah, but you're a Canadian.'

"A lot of Canadians don't think of me in the same terms as a Linda Ronstadt, Barbra Streisand or Olivia Newton John because I'm Canadian. They take you for granted."

As Ostick remarked, "This built-in Canadian tendency to downplay our home-grown heroes also might explain the inappropriate light-hearted attitude some took to Murray's problems with Saskatchewan farmer Robert Kieling. The 49-year-old bachelor has been sent to jail several times since 1984 for harassing Murray despite numerous court orders to stay away from her. Psychiatrists said Kieling suffers from an erotic paranoia in which he believes Murray is secretly in love with him. When the Snowbirds acrobatic team happened to fly over his farm, for instance, he took it as a signal from Murray.

" 'The first time I testified some people looked upon me as the wicked witch of the west doing this to this poor guy,' she said. 'I wasn't doing anything. I was just trying to get him to leave me alone. Canadians don't think about those kinds of things because it's not a violent country by and large. It would never occur to them that somebody might follow me and bug me. But you never know with these things; you don't dare take a chance. We haven't heard from him for a while, but in the past year everybody had to go to court and testify that he'd made hundreds of phone calls again.' "

Adding to the sense that there was sympathy for the farmer was the writing of a stage play which was launched in the unlikely setting of Thunder Bay, Ontario. The play was described by its producers as a Canadian vision of modern romantic obsession. Called *I Love You, Anne Murray*, it told Kieling's story up to the point where the two meet in a Toronto courtroom. According to news reports, "Although Thunder Bay seems an unlikely place to launch what promises to become a play of national interest, Theatre Magnus took on the job after artistic director Brian Richmond became fascinated with the story of farmer Robert Kieling's obsession with the singer. A spokesman for Murray said she won't be able to attend any of the performances of I Love You, Anne Murray which opened recently, but David Rimmer of Theatre Magnus said Kieling will travel from his Saskatchewan farm to take in one of the shows before it closes April 21."

According to an article in the *Toronto Star* on November 3, 1985, by E. Kaye Fulton, the trouble first began in 1971 when Murray made the innocent mistake of sending Kieling an autographed picture. "He's been besieging her ever since." In a story datelined Springhill, Fulton writes: "He walks purposefully up Main Street — up to the pale yellow house on top of the hill where Anne Murray grew up . . .

"He didn't bring the airplane ticket, the diamond ring or handfuls of wheat he once offered to Anne as gifts of affection. He carries no luggage. The only articles in his attaché case are a well-worn Bible and a copy of the Criminal Code.

"For Anne Murray does not love this troubled 49-year-old bachelor. In fact, she is afraid of him.

"As Kieling stands in the evening shadows on the Murray's front doorstep, the singer's mother, Marion, says, no, Anne is not there, and, no, she doesn't know where she is.

"He murmurs a polite thank-you and turns away.

"A dark blue Springhill police cruiser pulls to a stop alongside Kieling as he walks back down Main Street. The 10 police officers on the force know him well. After all these years, they consider him 'one of the boys.'

"He doesn't resist arrest. He doesn't argue. As one officer recalls later, he simply smiles, almost wearily, as he gets into the cruiser.

"And the bizarre and unsettling cycle in the private, tortured world of Robert Charles Kieling begins once again."

Kieling, it was well reported, had followed Murray across the country, showing up at her concerts, her Toronto office, her mother's home, and, according to one report, even her high school reunion. By the mid-1980s, Robert Charles Kieling had been in court more than 35 times over a period of approximately seven years. Dozens of charges later, he would not give up on his stubborn delusion that Murray was in love with him. As Bill Langstroth had once reported in the early *Singalong Jubilee* era of his acquaintanceship with Murray that she had been singing, it seemed, directly to him, Kieling too felt Murray was singing only to him and the message in the songs — the torment of love — was her way of conveying her caring. Langstroth, on the other hand, was not obsessed by Murray's voice, yet perhaps understood that for some it would have a seductive quality. And, obviously, as their marriage in 1975 proved, Langstroth and Murray's love was a mutual affair.

Kieling's passion, however, led him down a torturous road of running afoul of the law, of medical treatment and confinement, and of ignominious celebrity. His relentless stalking of Anne Murray put him in the public eye because she was one of this country's most famous performers. He spent, for example, a year in the Penetanguishene Mental Health Centre, known to be a psychiatric hospital for the criminally insane, located not far from Barrie, Ontario. There were additional periods in hospitals in Nova Scotia and back in Saskatchewan "because," as Fulton put it, "no one can convince him otherwise. Not the courts, not psychiatrists, not his sister, brother or mother. Not even Anne herself."

With respect to his legal transgressions, Kieling was convicted repeatedly of breaches of probation, defying court orders which prohibited him from contact with Murray or her family. The probation had been a result of his conviction in 1980 of a charge of intimidation. The charge carried a maximum sentence of six months in jail.

While Kieling's case ultimately reached the Supreme Court of Canada where a court-appointed lawyer attempted to get the Court to rule on whether prolonged incarceration in psychiatric hospitals — not only to be declared fit to stand trial but able to defend himself — infringed on his civil rights, the nature of his delusion was analyzed, sometimes sympathetically, sometimes not, always with an ultimate, hapless gesture of giving up.

The malady, in Kieling's case, seemed harmless enough. But it was not harmless to Murray who, in the public eye, was aware that there was a potential for danger. Kieling was often compared to

John Hinckley in the United States, the man who shot Ronald Reagan in March 1981, to prove his love for actress Jodie Foster. Although Kieling never showed any violent tendencies (there were reports that Murray was grabbed in concert as she bent down to a fan and that it was Kieling, an act one would consider violent or at least aggressive) the comparison still possessed a validity. And Murray, a willing signer of autographs, was aware of her right *not* to be stalked.

"Kieling has become an unwitting celebrity of sorts — this country's most obvious case of what is known as erotomania or erotic paranoia, a psychiatric disorder in which a person falls hopelessly in unrequited love with another, usually famous or prominent person, and chases them at any cost," wrote Fulton in 1985, precluding her own speculations on what in our society causes the delusion. "And though little is known about this guarded, private man or his illness, Kieling stands as a tragic exaggeration of the kind of emotionally destructive hero worship North American society spawns in the young, who live in a Walkman world of paper posters of a Springsteen, a Rambo or a Madonna. But the young grow up. Kieling is trapped in a grotesque adolescence that society cannot cope with."

Part of the difficulty in Kieling's case, however, was that he was *not* a John Hinckley, in the sense that it increased the puzzling nature of the case even while it seemed to diminish it. Certainly, this diminishing of the threat seemed to isolate Murray. As Kieling was portrayed sympathetically, especially in view of the helplessness of the authorities in dealing with his problem, what for Murray was a very real danger, and her actions to alleviate that danger, did, as she told Ostick, transform her into the "wicked witch of the west."

Some of the sympathy, however, was socially relevant. Said Fulton, "His unique case underlines a serious gap in Canada's legal and psychiatric systems: the legal network cannot protect the privacy of Anne Murray or her family, and the psychiatric world is seemingly powerless to help a man whose only crime stems, so far, from love." And back in Springhill, police chief Sam Macdonald was describing Kieling as "quiet, intelligent and he's a reader."

According to Fulton, Dr. Elliott Barker, a psychiatrist at Penetang who once testified that Kieling was "a textbook case of erotic para-noia," admitted there was not much optimism about treatment, despite psychotherapy or powerful antipsychotic tranquilizers. Fulton speculated that the death of Kieling's father in 1977 — "before the troubles began" (inconsistent with the story's assertion that the troubles had begun six years earlier than that with the autographed photograph) — might hold a clue to his psychologi-cal state. "Erotomania was first diagnosed in 1942 by French psy-chiatrist G.G. de Clerambault," said Fulton. "Since then, psychia-trists have linked its source to the loss or lack of fulfilling love and/or sexual relationships. Included in their list is the death of a father. Last year, a sympathetic play based on his cased added as much fiction as fact to his sad legend," said Fulton.

For example, it came to be believed, even by neighboring res-idents in Kieling's home in Blumenof, Saskatchewan, southeast of Swift Current, that Kieling and Murray were dating classmates in university. In fact, Kieling did not attend university, although he studied five courses by correspondence on his farm.

In 1985, after his latest transgression in Springhill, Kieling appeared in court on October 16 on his twelfth charge of breaking a court order. Apparently he argued that it was costly to taxpayers to keep him in jail while spring wheat crops on his two farms in Saskatchewan, damaged by hail, were rotting. Nonetheless, he was remanded to Cumberland Country Jail. Confinement in Cumberland County in Nova Scotia was not new to Kieling at the time. He had already served five months that same year in the Amherst jail on the same charge and, a year previously, he was in jail for four months.

"In each instance," wrote Fulton, "Kieling was ordered by the court to undergo a 30-day psychiatric assessment. Within a week of his release, he was back on Murray's doorstep, repeating the pattern that has frustrated police, angered the courts, frightened the Murray family and agonized his own.

"This obsession has endured for 14 years. In 1971, Kieling penned a fan letter to Anne Murray and enclosed a few seeds of wheat from his 260-hectare farm. The gift was acknowledged by a routine thank-you note, signed by Murray, who thought 'it was very nice.' "

It was in the period immediately afterwards that Kieling began to interpret her music and an assortment of other events — like the flying of the Snowbirds acrobatic team over his farm — as secret messages that she was beckoning him to her Toronto home. In addition, seeds of wheat were not the only item Kieling apparently sent to Murray to convince her of his love. He told his mother, Elizabeth, that he had sent her a diamond ring, suggesting that she must care for him because she did not return it. His mother reported that she had found a receipt for the ring on his dresser, reflecting a bill of approximately $500.

In view of the fact that such gifts to famous performers are not all that uncommon, there is no way to know whether Kieling's ring, if indeed it was sent, was ever returned or not. In Murray's case, however, George Anthony's *Chatelaine* article about her intention of having a private life, published in 1975, portrays a grim and unfortunate coincidence. According to Anthony, Leonard Rambeau and Murray are in her Toronto apartment and are deciding what Chinese food to order in

"Anne is about to tell me about the delicate ring she is wearing when she gets a brainstorm. 'Leonard!' she calls out. 'See if they have any of those long spareribs, will you?' He hollers an affirmative reply from the kitchen, and Anne lights another cigarette. The ring? Oh yeah, the ring. The ring is from a fan. Almost all her rings are from fans. 'I don't know when I've bought my own jewelry. Except for my turquoises.' One fan sent her a $400 diamond ring, and when customs asked her to pay $200 duty on it she sent it back to him, thanking him for the grand gesture. She got a card from him the following week, just part of her daily fan mail — except the diamond ring was taped to it. 'Imagine sending it through the mail.'

"Kids send her tons of stuff. 'I get a lot of bird plaques. Sketches, paintings. I've received an awful lot of birds in the last four years; kids make 'em, embroider 'em.' She also gets jokebooks and cookbooks — 'it's hard to know what to do with it all.' On her Arctic tour she admired a ring that a woman was wearing and the woman immediately took it off her finger and placed it on Anne's. 'I tried to refuse but she wouldn't hear of it, and I held back because I was afraid to offend her. Later when I really looked at it I realized that the ring has a jade centre surrounded by gold nuggets.' Another fan fashioned a silver pendant of the crest from Anne's LOVE SONG album."

Anthony's report on Murray's jewelry serves to outline the tenuous relationship between performers and their fans, tenuous because it conveys a sense of trust on both sides which is not always propitious. There can be misunderstandings, especially when a fan succumbs to an apparent delusion.

"He thinks I should be able to understand," Elizabeth Kieling, his mother, told Southam News back in 1985. "I said to him, 'This is what I understand, this is what's real. She has charged you, sent police after you and she isn't lifting a finger to get you out of trouble. And that tells me she doesn't care.'

"This thing is destroying my son. It isn't normal that he doesn't stop, we have to agree to that. But it's not a question now of whether he's right or wrong. It's a question of helping him."

Fulton also reported that "Kieling's single-minded obsession has branched into a dogged — and occasionally brilliant — quest to understand and beat the legal system that attempts to keep him at bay.

" 'He has his own idiosyncratic interpretations of the Criminal Code,' says Toronto lawyer Rebecca Shamai, who represented him on four occasions. 'But he is lucid and, at times, very convincing.'

"In an interview with Southam News in the Amherst jail last summer [1984], Kieling accurately recited sections of the code that pertained to his case. He discussed history, philosophy, law, religion — any subject but Anne Murray.

" 'Our relationship is private,' he said, bristling for the only time in an hour-long conversation. 'What we have is between the two of us. It's nobody else's business.' "

But whether or not Kieling would continue to defend himself and, on occasion, catch the court on points of law, the issue was difficult for Murray and her family. The performer who had staunchly defended her right to privacy was now quite literally fighting for another kind of privacy, one which would permit her and her family to live without fear.

At the same time, Kieling's mother was quick to point out at the time that he was not dangerous, painting a different portrait of her son. "The person who knows him best — and who says she often feels she does not know him at all — is his mother," wrote Fulton. "Kieling, asked the family not to speak to the media, but his mother broke her promise and talked to Southam News because she is heartbroken that his side of the story is untold.

" 'Nobody cares. They're putting him down across Canada. He is my son and he is worth caring about.'

"The only contact the family has had with authorities was a telephone call from a psychiatrist, asking Mrs. Kieling for permission to give her son drugs. Kieling, who accepts only aspirin, was being typically uncooperative. His mother refused.

" 'When you're with him, there's nothing wrong with him. He's quiet, he's generous. He's so normal. I think maybe she has given him some hope at some time. But he should know by now that she doesn't care."

The Fulton article portrayed Kieling as something other than a dangerous stalker, acknowledging that his Blumenof home was filled with photographs of Anne Murray, despite the fact he would only talk about her with his mother. Other things known about him was his penchant for classical music, the fact he briefly studied guitar and taught himself German and French, plus the fact he was not interested in any particular girl, especially because girls were limited in numbers in his small village of residence. One more thing, he apparently had a passion for hockey and later coached a minor league team.

"As an adult," wrote Fulton, "he gives 'thousands of dollars' each year to charities, such as the Christian Blind Mission and UNICEF. His mother knows this because she is in charge of his mail while he is in jail. Otherwise, he never mentions it.

"He worked hard to save enough money to buy and develop a 260-hectare farm in Blumenof and another 65 acres he inherited from his father. During his lengthy absences — he'd often slip away without telling anyone — his sister and her husband tend the farms. They say he always pays them when he returns, and pays them well.

" 'I want to tell you one more thing about Charles,' said Mrs. Kieling. 'You know, he never imposed on me or his sister or his neighbors. Frankly, we can't understand that he would impose on this woman. It's not his nature. He told me he would give up if Anne sent back his letters and the diamond ring. I wonder. But they're backing him into corners he can't get out of.

" 'I'm a Christian. I grew up in a Christian home but we're not fanatical about it. But I pray that the Lord would send him a woman, one who would really appreciate him and love him. He is alone too much.

" 'And he does need love.' "

Over the years since then, the Kieling issue has dissipated but the questions it raises have not, about the nature of the delusion, about the relationship between performers and their audiences, about what a performer's right to privacy actually is in the face of an adulation which determines the extent of their livelihood, and how an unfortunate circumstance becomes a major topic because one half of the conflict is a major musical star.

For a long time, Charles Kieling was routinely part of interviews with Murray. He shows up, for example, in Elspeth Cameron's 1988 article on Murray, three years later.

"Many people responded to that curious mix of spiritual and sensual ecstasy in Anne's voice," wrote Cameron. "Robert Charles Kieling, a Saskatchewan farmer not much older than Anne, thought she was singing to him. 'At the beginning, he was on a religious kick,' Rambeau recalls. But before long he wanted to tie Anne down on a table and caress her downy thighs. 'My *downy thighs*, for gawd's sake!' was her comment. Murray's lawyer was soon after Kieling to stop his harassment, but Kieling is *still* hot on the trail, even after several months in jail and attempts by Anne to talk him out of his erotomania. In the first four months of this year, he had phoned her office 188 times."

The underside of fame and fortune. The conflict between the right to privacy and earning one's income from a worshipful public. And all of it brought home to Springhill where the breakfast club meets and refills your cup and where, barely two hundred yards away, the Anne Murray Centre is located to provide visitors to the town with a blow-by-blow of Murray's achievements. Kieling has no place of honor here where visitors are mostly seeking "a little good news."

Not surprisingly, some of the other conflicts in which Murray took part are not mentioned inside its doors either. But when Anne Murray decided to say her piece, Springhill's famous daughter said her piece, regardless of the issue. The Juno Awards, Canadian content regulations, and, of course, the always inviting controversy over her changing image.

The album cover of WHERE DO YOU GO WHEN YOU DREAM? *portrays two sides of Anne's character in a playful manner.*

Anne hugs her first of many Grammy awards for Best Performance by a Female Country Vocalist.

Anne receives her award as Number One Adult Contemporary Artist in 1980 from Billboard *magazine.*

CHAPTER NINE

That's Not The Way It's S'posed To Be

My career could have taken many different directions over the years. I'm really an old rock and roller at heart, but I started off having success with ballads, and you don't look a gift horse in the mouth. . . . I've always contended that if you're a good singer, you can sing anything. If that's tough these days, then I'll get tough. — Anne Murray

Anne Murray's hosting of the 1996 Juno Awards ceremony in Hamilton served to complete one of the most well-known circles of controversy in Canadian music history. While the awards celebrated their twenty-fifth anniversary, so did Murray who received her first Juno Award at the first ceremonies in 1971 for *Snowbird*. In a very real sense, the rise of Canadian music to international status corresponds to the rise of Anne Murray's star. For many, her role as host was ironical. For she had once been a vocal critic of the lack of quality of the Juno Awards which led her to boycott the events during much of the late 1970s and early 1980s. Canada's premier music awards show was one well-known instance where Murray decided to state her case. And when she did, there was a resounding backlash from which she did not back down.

"Murray wasn't considered much of a sport within Canadian music circles after refusing to attend the Juno Awards for 12 years until 1986, despite racking up 28 wins," writer Steve Ostick reported approximately a decade ago. "She said the show was poor quality.

" 'That show was a travesty,' she said. 'I hadn't worked all these years to go on there and look like a fool.

" 'They've worked really hard to try and make it right and I was real proud of them last year when I went. For a lot of years, it was just, 'Canadian music awards? Who cares?' Well it's not that way now. They mean something.' "

Murray had been top winner at the Juno Awards in 1980, winning in four categories which, at the time, brought her career total to sixteen. The amassing of awards at the Juno ceremonies for Murray was so staggering that the *Toronto Sun* quipped that maybe the award should be renamed the "Annies." But Murray reported that she was exasperated by what she considered the technical sloppiness of the show and told broadcaster Peter Gzowski that the final straw was when Ed Schreyer could not be heard over the noise of the crowd while he was trying to make a dedication to the late pianist Glenn Gould.

Reports revealed that Murray would never again appear on the Junos until people showed proper respect or until the technical problems which bothered her were corrected. As Virginia Beaton and Stephen Peterson pointed out in *Maritime Music Greats*, "Murray told organizers that when they cleaned up the show and found somebody who could light and shoot her properly, she'd be back."

A report in the *Globe & Mail* in late 1984 showed little indication that the issue was going to be easily resolved. "Murray, whose absence last year from the Juno Awards was criticized by Vancouver talent manager Bruce Allen, said she was unsure if she would attend next month's Juno ceremony. . . . The 1983 ceremony was 'awful, worse than the year before,' she said.

" 'I was embarrassed for Gordon Lightfoot. I was embarrassed for the Canadian music industry. I had to turn down the sound (on the television). It was terrible.' "

It was, by now, a trait of Murray's that she could readily be critical of an event which did not suit her powerful sense of organization or professionalism, something she had demonstrated early in her career, as far back as the early 1970s. "At a confused press reception staged for her in Halifax by Capitol Records, Anne was asked what kinds of things bother her most. 'Things like this,' she replied bluntly, as a Capitol executive shifted uneasily nearby. 'This is poorly organized.' "

What made the Juno issue even more controversial was some of the response by other notables in the Canadian music business. For one thing, it was suggested that Murray should consider withdrawing from the Best Female Vocalist category, where she was inevitably a winner, simply to give someone else a chance. When she refused, Bruce Allen, manager of Bryan Adams (and now Murray's manager too), attempted to get her to return, pointing out that Canadian entertainers had some kind of duty to show up at the biggest awards ceremony the Canadian music industry offers.

As Perry Stern commented: "Things being what they are, there have been a few controversies over the years. By 1981 Anne had become the full-blown Canadian equivalent to Mom and Apple Pie, so when she put her foot down and refused to appear on the perennially amateurish Juno Awards TV show (while at the same time refusing the absurd suggestion that she withdraw her name from the Best Female Artist category to give someone a shot at breaking her strangle-hold on the award) a tempest in a tea-pot broke out.

" 'I was real adamant about that,' she says, even now getting agitated about the 'scandal'. 'They crapped on me enough. I wasn't going to take a stand, and then I thought, Forget it. It's a shitty television show, it's embarrassing, so don't tell me I should do it.' Soon Bruce Allen, Bryan Adams' outspoken manager out in Vancouver, was raising hell. 'I think Bruce Allen was trying to make a point and who better to pick on than me because he was going to get a reaction. It worked great.'

" 'He had a good point that if you're in Canadian show business, then you should show up on these things because how can we make it a legit show that people are going to watch if the biggest people in the business won't show up. Well, that was a legitimate point, it sure was, and I was never angry at him, though I think he may have thought I was. I was just angry at the whole situation that somebody would expect me to go someplace when I thought it was beneath me to do it. I don't think it was uppity or snobby or anything. It was realistic. And so it was great the way it all happened because Bruce started something and the wheels started to move and it's all worked out.' Once she felt the TV show was up to professional standards, Anne again returned to the fold."

And, reported Beaton and Peterson, "Eventually the show was redesigned. It now takes place in a more subdued theater setting with no eating or drinking during the awards. Murray admitted to Gzowski that upon her return to the fold she was mildly nervous about what kind of reception she'd get. But she was greeted with a standing ovation."

Over the years, however, the Juno Awards have endured other slights, some of them very subtle, as entertainment acts have dismissed them, condemning them to some unrealistic comparison with the American Grammys. When Heart was awarded a Juno in the early years — they were an American band which first made it in Canada, moving from Seattle to Vancouver — three members of the group, excluding the Wilson sisters without whom there would be no group, accepted the award. One of them quipped, "Anybody want a Juno?" as he accepted the award. The ingrate's slap in the face was obvious — this was simply Canada and, when a star was on the wax, what difference did tribute from Canada make?

But as Murray herself pointed out to Stern, Bruce Allen had a point. And perhaps she did too, especially in view of the technical faults of the program during its years of fledgling development, and most especially in view of the suggestion that she should withdraw to give other female performers a chance. This, most of all, was insulting in view of her talent and success in national as well as international music circles.

But at the same time there was a larger issue at play here, the equally perennial, indeed unending implication that the United States defines Canadian culture and musical success. Although not specifically from Murray's lips or from Bruce Allen's or from any-one else's, was it possible that the Juno's were technically flawed only by comparison with the Grammys? And those who were concerned about their "amateurish" appearance, were they not contrasting them with the so-called more professional Grammys? In other words, were the Junos symbolic of a Canadian music industry which must be judged exclusively by its larger and more powerful American counterpart?

Canadian *Billboard* editor Larry LeBlanc feels that some American Country Music Award programs, even those hosted by Murray in the past, were on a par with the maligned Junos. And he maintains that Murray had been asked to host the Junos back then and had enough clout to see about the improvements herself, without backing out of the ceremonies. "If anybody could have changed the CBC it would have been Anne Murray," he said. "They asked her to be host. She could have changed it in a minute."

At the same time there was a question about whether the Junos were a poor cousin simply because the achievements of Canadians musically on a much larger international scale were becoming only newly more frequent. One can speculate, for example, that the awards might have been more palatable to per-formers with reputations limited to inside Canadian borders. But as performers gained international acclaim, the Junos were going to find it difficult to compete with the glamor of a Grammy, even to superstars like Murray and Bryan Adams who chose to honor their Canadianism.

To the credit of the Juno voters, despite Murray's continuing boycott in the early 1980s, she continued to take the award home to such an extent that the *Toronto Sun's* remark that they could be renamed the "Annie's" seemed almost a serious proposal. And this fact demonstrated that the program was willing to rise above the flak of her criticism while, at the same time, was prepared to acknowledge her great talent and success. And now that she is a lifetime Juno Award winner, the Canadian music industry is glad the tempest in a teapot is over.

It was during the 1993 Juno Awards televised live from Hamilton on March 21 that the singer's 25th anniversary as a recording star was marked as she was inducted into the Canadian Music Hall of Fame, where she joined such luminaries as Leonard Cohen, Maureen Forrester, The Band, The Guess Who, Gordon Lightfoot, Wilf Carter, Glenn Gould, Neil Young, Joni Mitchell, Paul Anka, Hank Snow, Oscar Peterson, and Guy Lombardo.

"The event's sponsor," the Canadian Press reported, "the Canadian Academy of Recording Arts and Sciences, says in a release that with a total of 26 RPM and Juno awards, Murray holds the all-time record. The Nova Scotia-born vocalist also holds a clutch of international awards, including four Grammys, three American Music Awards and three Country Music Awards. Over the last quarter century, Murray's 30-plus record albums have had worldwide sales of more than 24 million."

No wonder that Anne Murray received another standing ovation at the 1996 awards presentation, this one too indicating that all was forgiven. The Canadian music industry is a small circle of acquaintances and there would be other controversies which would develop. No sooner had Murray resolved the Junos controversy when she was involved with another one, although, according to reports, it was worked out very quickly.

During the recording of *Tears Are Not Enough*, the amalgamation of all the premier Canadian musical artists to raise funds for famine-plagued Africa, Bryan Adams, one of the prime movers of the project with producer David Foster, complained about Murray's insistence that her brother, Bruce, be on the recording. After disagreeing on the subject, the two stars talked about it and the issue was resolved.

Larry LeBlanc, who has taped hours of interviews with Adams, explains, "Bryan's a purist. He felt it was nepotism." In the end, however, Bruce Murray appears on the recording. According to LeBlanc. "He's [Bruce Murray] a real nice guy. They [Anne Murray and Adams] talked about it at the session."

And Murray showed them what a superstar can do when it comes to working in the studio. As Liam Lacey reported in *The Globe & Mail* in 1985: "Some indication of that concentration was given during the taping of *Tears Are Not Enough*, the famine-relief song performed by Canadians, when Murray sang her line perfectly the first time. The producer, David Foster, came 'on the blower', she says. 'He was laughing, and he asked me if I wanted to do it again. I said, 'Why?' But we did it again, and it was almost exactly the same, though the first one was a shade better. We went with the first one, and he said, 'How can you do that?' I told him I've had 15 years' practice.' "

The issue over Bruce Murray's presence on the famine-relief recording is noteworthy only in that it drives home how small the music industry and its membership really is and the resulting ironies which can take place. A number of years later Murray came out slugging in Adams' corner over Canadian content regulations, and most recently was in the studio with Adams preparing a duet for her next album, not to mention already sharing management with him, the aforementioned Bruce Allen with whom she had taken a different view over the Junos. Of even more interest, where irony is concerned, Murray was exposed to the production techniques of David Foster, but when he produced a song for her on her album SOMETHING TO TALK ABOUT, it would contribute to more controversy because the effort was seen as outside the parameters of her style.

Once again, Murray was outspoken over the recent Canadian content issue. "Recording superstars Gordon Lightfoot and Anne Murray have backed rocker Bryan Adams' demand that the federal government get out of the music business," said a Canadian Press story which appeared in many national media.

" 'He's a freakin' hero!' Murray said here [dateline Toronto]. 'They should be playing the hell out of him, instead of putting limits on him.'

"Lightfoot said Adams was 'courageous to say something at last.

" 'I've had many an opportunity to expound on this issue over the years and I didn't. Maybe I've been worried about retribution.'

"At a news conference in Sydney, N.S., Adams criticized Canadian content regulations, saying they bred mediocrity. The following report appeared in the press.

"The Canadian Radio-television and Telecommunications Commission caused a furore last year (1991) by ruling songs on his latest album, WAKING UP THE NEIGHBOURS, didn't qualify as Canadian content because they were co-written and produced by Britain's Mutt Lange.

"It meant the songs were limited to 18 playings per week on Canadian FM radio stations.

" 'I realize we have to have some kind of regulations to support the industry, but we have to take a good hard look at how far we go,' Murray said.

" 'I've had the same problem for years,' said Murray, who has had a number of albums that didn't qualify as Canadian content under the current rules.

"Music industry representatives defended the rules Tuesday, but noted a minor change is needed to reflect the increasing amount of collaboration between Canadian and non-Canadian songwriters.

"Lightfoot said he agrees with Adams that the Canadian content rule 'has turned into something that it shouldn't. It still takes talent to make a hit, and in that respect I think it is redundant.'

"However, other homegrown musicians disagreed.

"Pop singer Andrew Cash said he has 'a hard time feeling sorry' for Adams and argued the rules help protect Canadians 'from the dominant culture living right next door.

" 'In Germany, all they play is American music and they don't even speak English.'

"Allan Frew, singer with the rock group Glass Tiger, said the content rules do not provide 'a free ride' for Canadian musicians because radio stations know how to break the rules.

" 'I think it's a great help to Canadian acts and I support it,' said Frew, whose band had an international hit in the late '80s with the song *Don't Forget Me (When I'm Gone)*.

" 'I think Canadian content has really, really helped the industry,' said drummer Gil Moore, formerly of defunct hard rock trio Triumph.

" 'Cancon is not something that's going to make the difference between a hit and a stiff. It's not a flawless system by any means,' he said.

" 'Bryan Adams is in a situation where they say he's not Canadian content and obviously he's Canadian. But is it really hurting him? Is he selling any fewer records?' "

In spite of Murray's plain talk in the controversy, it paled in significance to what continued to be the most regularly controversial item in her career — changes of image. It wasn't long after her introduction to the work of fellow Canadian producer David Foster that the latest round of argument about her image would take place.

As Larry LeBlanc sees it, Murray is in a peculiar position with respect to her Canadian fans. He blames it on the fact she was a television star before she was a music star. "There's no distance with Anne, we all feel we know her." And, of course, we don't. Which most of her image changes have driven home. No matter how uncomfortable it felt to discover it, when Anne Murray changed her look, her style and dabbled in somewhat different genres of music other than those in which we had her pigeonholed, we objected fiercely.

As Perry Stern has documented: "The next so-called controversy was her attempt in 1986 to shed, once again, her country label by overhauling her visual as well as her musical image. For some reason people look at the release of SOMETHING TO TALK ABOUT as a failure, but if it was it was only a failure conceptually, not financially or in terms of her career. Using David Foster on *Now and Forever*, media pundits claimed, was a cynical attempt to get back on the pop charts. In fact it was just another in a series of alternating directions that her career had always taken. Rambeau laughs at the outcome now. 'When we wanted to do a country album [LET'S KEEP IT THAT WAY in 1978 with *You Needed Me* on it] we had a number one Pop hit. When we went to do a blatantly pop record we ended up with a number one country song [*Now And Forever*].' If radio programmers who thought the three quarter million selling album was a failure, he adds, 'then they didn't hear the hits, but they weren't getting the royalty statements either.' "

Or, to put it another way, Rambeau asked, "How many other people's mistakes sell 750,000 units?"

But if Murray was showing some ambivalence about the kind of material she wished to sing, she was also pragmatically aware of where her success had traditionally rested. She had, throughout her career, labored steadfastly to rid herself of the label of purely country artist and her pop success had demonstrated that she had succeeded. Still, on those occasions when she moved more closely to rock, a rather stern Canadian media typically professed its disapproval.

For Murray, the response was to the point. As she told Liam Lacey: "My career could have taken many different directions over the years. I'm really an old rock and roller at heart, but I started off having success with ballads, and you don't look a gift horse in the mouth . . . I've always contended that if you're a good singer, you can sing anything. If it's that tough these days, then I'll get tough."

Lacey asked her if she had ever had a great record that wasn't a great song and she thought about it a moment before replying. "No, I don't think so. There are some songs I'd want to do over again but, for their time, they were done well. They're not all regular songs; *You Needed Me*, which is one of the two really big records of my career — along with *Snowbird* — is pretty unusual as a song. It doesn't really have a chorus. I had to plead with the president of Capitol Records to release it as a single. I knew in the studio what it was. I just had this shudder down my spine when I was singing it."

Lacey also reported that Murray also had one more criticism at the time with which she wished to dispense. "From time to time people say I don't have much of a range, which is really stupid. You just have to *listen* to know that's not true. My range is about two and half octaves — and I could probably push it up to three with falsetto — which is what most of the good ones have. I suppose people aren't as impressed because I sound relaxed but, you know, I'm working just as hard to sound relaxed as other singers are to sound strained."

The collective Canadian gasp when SOMETHING TO TALK ABOUT was released had more than one tangent to it. For one thing, the cover sported a rather glamorous, albeit black and white, photograph of Murray in a miniskirt and jacket with padded shoulders. Wait a minute, were Canadian *apple*hood and *mother*pie singers supposed to have legs like that? Murray, it should be noted, has always had a frankly appreciative regard for her own legs. A youthful photograph in David Livingstone's pictorial festival in 1981 is captioned, "but great legs, though." And there have been media references over the years that her clothes were often designed to make the most of her legs.

The most amusing aside, though, is George Anthony's 1975 *Chatelaine* article which begins in the following way: "We bump into each other in the hall. Anne is wearing a smashing, figure-hugging knee-length dress and a new Afro-chic hairstyle, and she looks sensational. She has come to do *The Entertainers*, a half-hour talk show on Global TV, on which she will be the sole guest and I will be her host.

" 'Hiya,' she drawls, satin-pink lips sliding lazily into that easy grin. She stops in her tracks and hikes up her skirt to reveal some surprising curves. 'Thought I'd give you as much leg as possible, George — I know how you like that sorta thing.' She ignores my bulging eyeballs and sails past me into makeup, where a clutch of autographs are waiting to be signed after Roger Palmer gives her a last-minute touch up. Leonard Rambeau, Anne's manager, taps me lightly on the shoulder.

" 'I hope you realize,' he says soberly, 'that this is quite an event.'

" 'Oh I do, I do,' I assure him quickly. 'I realize Anne doesn't do this sort of interview show as a rule, and I do appreciate it, Leonard, really I do.'

" 'Not the *show*,' says Rambeau, a master at deadpan delivery. 'The *legs*. It's the first time any of us have seen her legs in four years!.' He smiles slyly. Big city boy that I am, I have taken the Maritime bait again, and swallowed it whole."

Still, there it was on the cover of SOMETHING TO TALK ABOUT, some Canadian glamor to talk about. The updated image caused a bit of a furore which was only exaggerated once people listened to the LP in general and *Now And Forever* in particular.

At the time, *Now And Forever* had all the essential components for success. The song, after all, was a composition by David Foster, Jim Vallance (Bryan Adams' old song-writing partner), and Randy Goodrum, author of *You Needed Me*. Never mind that Foster's material and, especially, Foster's production had a tendency to become so *Fosterish* as to make the lead vocalist interchangeable.

When SOMETHING TO TALK ABOUT *was* first released, however, there were those who were enthusiastic about it. Critic Wilder Penfield III, for example, suggested it had much to recommend it. "More muscle is flexed inside than ever before by an Anne Murray team. And this team is new with a physical fit, young at heartfelt approach that conjures up visions of dancing in the studio. . . . So it is no surprise that CHUM was quick to join the more conservative Murray boosters on the dial. The surprise is that the conservatives have not fallen by the wayside.

"Although her continuing presence is a sign of what has been happening to easy listening radio she may now also be important to its future. And while Foster was obviously hired to give her a rock thrust, she is returning the favor by giving him his first country hit — next week *Now And Forever* enters American country's top 100 at number fifty-eight. . . .

"But the stylishness of both the singing and the sound continues to make this the Anne Murray album of the '80s.

" 'Maybe it was turning 40 that did it,' Anne said yesterday on the phone from New York. 'This is the first album my kids are real excited about. Suddenly I had to find two Walkmans yesterday so they could both take it to school with them.'

"Eleven months in the making, SOMETHING TO TALK ABOUT is the album she has been *talking* about making for at least five years longer. 'Many producers didn't want the responsibility of taking me *over the edge*,' she says with an easy laugh.

"She downplayed the risks then and she downplays the risk now. 'My mother likes it,' she reports. 'It's not going to turn anyone off.' "

But a year later, Murray herself would be "turned off" by the experiment. "The only thing that hasn't lived up to Murray's standards recently was last year's David Foster-produced recording, SOMETHING TO TALK ABOUT," wrote James Muretich in the *Calgary Herald*. "A stab at the pop market after years of being seen largely as a country music artist, Murray admits the disc was not something to talk about.

" 'Musically, I had just been balladed to death and I wanted to break out of that, which was what I tried on that album. If the album didn't succeed it might've been because the material wasn't as good as mine normally is.

" 'Technically, I've never sang better and I think my new album, HARMONY, will be an improvement because the songs are better. I've always been able to hear hits and I feel I've got at least four good hit songs on the upcoming album,' says Murray."

Reporter Beth Gorham, in a long profile in a 1987 Halifax *Chronicle-Herald* article, also discussed the experiment with Murray. "HARMONY, said Murray, 'is the same sort of stuff I've done through the '70s. . . . This one I pulled the reins in a bit and used some real instruments. I'm getting a little tired of synthesizers.

" 'If I had a criticism of the last album, it was that it was a little clinical, cold and, you know, the tracks were all done in Munich . . . and sent to me and I put on the vocals. But I really think anybody's voice could have gone on them. The way I like to do albums is you go in the studio with the musicians and my voice is an integral part of the whole process from day one. I think that makes a big difference.' "

Part of the difficulty of the music business by the mid-1980s was the frequency of change, not only in trend, but in technology. And there were economic factors to be considered as well. The music business was changing radically in many ways and, if Murray was to be in the vanguard of these changes, or at least not left behind by them, she had the courage to attempt to make changes.

Where *Now and Forever* was concerned, at least some of the

controversy surrounded the accompanying video. For Canadian fans who had witnessed the youthful singer on *Singalong Jubilee*, had heard her recording career incorporate *Snowbird, Danny's Song*, and *You Needed Me*, it was relatively daunting to deal with a visual Anne Murray in a video, miniskirted, with bleached and spiked blonde hair, kissing a strange man on an elevator. But the music business was now focusing on videos. Technology had moved into the music industry, not only in the form of film, but in the studio as well.

These were not the only changes to take place. Harsh economic factors were having their impact on the music industry as well. By the mid-1980s, Murray, like most of her peers, was faced with the economic realities of touring. While her appearances in Canada became less frequent — due to her insistence that she employ a work schedule which reflected the importance she placed on being a wife and mother, as well as the logistics of travel and economics — Murray began to tour the United States with more frequency than Canada, simply because the distances between appropriate concert settings and performance venues were less arduous. Time and workload required to transport musicians, technical crew, and all the others involved in a performance by a musical performer of Murray's stature were, at times, almost overwhelming.

As for economics, costs of mounting a concert tour for Murray and other major stars were becoming prohibitive. Even in Las Vegas, promoters were turning to less expensive performers. Murray was not alone when the issue of corporate sponsorship entered the realm of music performance. A wide variety of artists endured criticism when they began to permit corporate sponsors of their tours to help underwrite the ever-increasing costs.

As Perry Stern again noted, "The final controversy brewed up in 1987. For the first time in her career she decided to mount a cross-Canada tour. An expensive proposition for even the smallest outfit. Anne had long learned that it was prohibitively so for her large stage show. Ford came in as her corporate sponsor.

"'That was a big, big tour for me,'" she remembers. 'It was an unusual situation. Canada's a difficult place to tour. The cities are so far apart. I can go play in New York State for months and every night I can play in a place that has 50,000 people. It's unbelievable to me because where I come from you drive a hundred miles and you find a place where there's 500 people, then you drive another 50 miles and there's another 500 people. In New York, every time I play there I play in a city I've never heard of and they say, Oh yeah, there's 150,000 people here! In Canada you've gotta get on a plane with twenty other people everytime you turn around. That's a lot of hotels and a very expensive venture which is precisely the reason I never did it before.' "

Enter Ford and the criticism following along just behind it. Which was when Murray responded, "No one gives a shit whether I'm sponsored by Ford." Beaton and Peterson, in *Maritime Music Greats*, took the view that such sponsorship was inevitable. "Rising costs were affecting all aspects of the music business, and corporate production of tours was the only solution. Soloists who had once carried large bands and backup singers on tour were having to cut back, partly because they couldn't manage the expenses associated with hotels, transportation and salaries. And with the advent of electronic keyboards, programming and synthesizers, it was possible to reduce bands even farther since one musician could cover several instrumental parts by duplicating the sounds on a keyboard. Audiences didn't always like so much electronic edge to the sound. They complained that it was often too loud and that unlike the good old days of players who could show off by improvising a new solo each night, drum machines and dense electric sounds made every band sound alike. But it was often much easier for the music arranger and director. A synthesizer, some argued, is utterly reliable, costs less to transport, and never takes an extended coffee break or asks for more money."

As the second decade of Anne Murray's triumphant career continued to unfold, she continued to produce, despite the fierce trend changes which took place in virtually every aspect of the music industry. She had also spoken out on a variety of issues and had not backed down. Most of all, however, she had shown she would perpetually be her own person. When Paul Anka penned *My Way* for Frank Sinatra, he might have more accurately defined Anne Murray. It was now clear to most Canadians that Murray intended to do things her way, perhaps always had.

AN EVENING WITH

Anne Murray

MUSICAL CONDUCTOR – PAT RICCIO JR.

PAT RICCIO, JR., Piano
PETER CARDINALI, Bass/Arranger
JORN ANDERSEN, Drummer/Vocals
AIDAN MASON, Guitar/Vocals
BRIAN GATTO, Organ/Accordian/Steel Guitar/Synthesizer
GEORGE HEBERT, Guitar
BUTCH WATANABE, Trombone/Mouth Organ
DAVID CALDWELL, Sax/Flute
CHARLES GRAY, Trumpet
BRUCE MURRAY, Vocals
DEBORAH GREIMANN, Vocals

LOREDANA FLEBBE, Violin
WOLFGANG FLEBBE, Violin
RUTH HOFFMAN, Violin
HENRY KRICHKER, Violin
SHMUEL GLAZMAN, Violin
INGA LAWRENCE, Violin
BEVERLY GROVE, Violin
FREDERICK ALLT, Violin
STEVEN WEDELL, Viola
YVONNE DEROLLER, Viola
MARY KANNER, Viola
NORMA LEE BISHA, Viola
SHIMON WALT, Cello
EITAN CORNFIELD, Cello
JAMES FARADAY, Percussion
DON PALMER, Sax/Flute/Clarinet
DANIEL MARTIN, Trombone

STEPHEN LEWIS, Production Manager
MAURICE CARDINAL, Road Manager
STEPHEN PAQUETTE, Stage Manager
PAUL DEVILLIERS, Audio Engineer
BRUCE DRYSDALE, Stage Technician
SHEILA YAKIMOV, Hairdresser
GEORGE ABBOTT, Make-up Artist
JUUL HAALMEYER DESIGNS, Costumes

LEONARD T. RAMBEAU, Personal Manager

BALMUR LTD., SUITE 412, 4881 YONGE STREET, TORONTO, ONTARIO M2N 5X3

ANNE MURRAY

"To everything she sings, she brings an aptness of phrasing and an intelligence of manner that are very appealing. She also happens to have a very beautiful voice. Miss Murray is a fine singer...she is a veritable princess of taste and style" — NEW YORK TIMES

"For some reason, my attention was caught by the audience. They were spellbound. They were totally caught up in what she was doing. It takes a rather important talent to make that happen." — PHOENIX PROGRESS

"In a business where "hype", the process of making someone or something larger than life is thought to be the key to success, Anne has frustrated the hypers. She is everything they say; she is more" — LAS VEGAS SUN

"Anne Murray, a Canadian singer who has been emphatically labelled country as she has pop...She has one of the widest range potentials among females in contemporary music. And that has nothing to do with either her range as a vocalist or her power as a performer...It is her honesty and superb musicianship that makes her a true soul singer of the middle of the road. Even the difficult to please hard rock critics have warmed to her totally unpretentious way with a song. But Murray is one singer who is almost impossible to criticize" — LOS ANGELES HERALD EXAMINER.

MARITIME TOUR '82

Anne Murray's tours of the Maritimes are always seen as homecoming celebrations.

Special thanks to Management and Staff of the Metro Centre, Aitken Centre, Coliseum, 92 CJCH, CKCW, CFQM, CIHI, CFNB, duMaurier Council for the Performing Arts, Capitol Records-EMI of Canada

CHAPTER TEN

Blessed Are The Believers

I've had a really good career, but quite frankly I'd rather be a well-rounded human being than a well-rounded performer . . . One thing I've always had is common sense, and a lot of people have found it boring. But it's kept me alive.

— Anne Murray

By the end of the 1980s, Anne Murray was quite literally calling her own tune. She had found the way to balance an extremely successful career with a very private private life. Murray had undergone a number of changes in her life, coinciding with an always rising career. For most Canadians, she was now an institution, a household name, an ideal version of ourselves we could understand. It was as if Anne Murray represented all the virtues Canadians feel reflect success. She was a loyal Canadian, a woman with a focus on her family, and a reluctant entertainer who fiercely clung to her private life. With her stardom, both at home and abroad, now guaranteed, no one was paying much attention to the fact that her career had already apparently peeked in the late 1970s. As an audience, we clung to the popular notions of our favorite musical star. As Elspeth Cameron put it in *Chatelaine*, "There's the glitzy show-biz Anne who wows 'em at Vegas and wins all those awards, and who's been Canada's favorite pop star for 20 years. Then there's the private Anne — fond wife and mother, shrewd businesswoman and strong-willed rebel."

And we delighted in recounting her achievements, offsetting these with her role of wife and mother. "Anne Murray is a phenomenon, all right, but she is neither naive nor a coal miner's daughter, and her success wasn't exactly a piece of cake," said Cameron. "There is no denying her success, however. She has sold out Carnegie Hall in New York, the Royal Albert Hall and the Palladium in London, England; the O'Keefe Centre and the Royal Alexandra Theatre in Toronto. She is right up there atop the pinnacle of fame, with Barbra Streisand her only real competition for best female pop singer in the world. She has won more than 100 major pop and country awards, and more Junos than any other Canadian. She has silver, gold and platinum records from around the globe — even from the Philippines and Japan. She has attained this dizzying height without sacrificing her marriage to Bill Langstroth. Or missing out on parenting her two children, William and Dawn."

We thought we knew who we were dealing with. Not only had Murray managed to turn a career with a short life expectancy into a long-term creation of 20 years (and it would be longer still), but she had managed to survive the demands on a private life such a career can create. Behind her were the bad periods when, lost in the glitter in the wake of recording hit records, of seeking a successful professional image, she had nearly lost sight of herself and what her personal ambitions were. Gone was the performer who had threatened more than once to retire from show business, who had continued to seem a trifle reluctant to go on, especially when she was on the verge of climbing the next dynamic step towards superstardom.

Although later she would admit that she always suspected her dream of singing with the likes of Perry Como would work out in the end, a fact she kept secret when she was young, there had been a serious ambivalence about whether or not to keep going. Her reluctance to even attend the second audition for *Singalong Jubilee*, the invitation offered by Bill Langstroth, her resisting of the invitations to make music her full-time career, again by Langstroth and Brian Ahern, her down period after the surprising success of *Snowbird*, the long gap between this hit and the next pair, *Danny's Song* and *Love Song*, her sampling of various images designed to turn her into someone other than who she really was, all of these things had shown that Anne Murray wasn't quite sure whether to keep going or not.

But as she said during the period of superstardom which commenced with the hit song *You Needed Me*, it came together for her with her marriage to Langstroth in 1975 and the birth of her first child, William, many months later. It was then, having discovered her need for a rewarding private life, her courage to demand that she be able to live it and the ability to juggle this life with a newfound need to pursue her career, that Anne Murray became the private and somewhat elusive "Anne Murray" that she was apparently meant to be.

Often Murray has stated her preference for the nurturing side of her nature rather than the performing side. In this way, she was able to go on with the fiercely demanding career of entertainer and singer. Only after she and Langstroth embarked on their family together was she able to shrug off the mystification she felt at having once been a small-town girl from Springhill, Nova Scotia, who was suddenly cast into the international limelight where it was expected she wanted only to be a star.

Ultimately that was the key. All the while that Murray did not want to be a star, Murray wanted to be a star. But we weren't necessarily going to know that for sure. There was going to be a side of Anne Murray which would belong entirely to her and her family. And the career would, like a passenger jammed into the front seat of the car, ride along as a guest in whichever direction the driver wished to go. By the beginning of her second decade of stardom, Murray had established certain principles. First of all, she would live in Canada. In addition, although she would continue to "bust her buns" where her career was concerned, she would work her own schedule, a schedule built around the importance of her family. For years now, Murray has lived up to this commitment by maintaining a work schedule of two weeks on and two weeks off, to permit her to spend more time with her children. She continues to maintain her bond with Nova Scotia, especially during the summer months, vacationing while other performers are working. She continues to sustain her non-musical interests, sports such as tennis and golf and swimming, in an attempt to live her life on an even keel. And if this means she can't be completely defined by her audience as one kind of cliche or another — either an aggressive careerist or a down-home girl wrenched into reluctant stardom — well that's just fine with her.

As she told writer James Uretich, "You get sick and tired of the people who are in *People* magazine every two weeks. I think my low profile over the years has helped. Certainly, outside of Canada, I haven't over-saturated the market. I don't lead a show business life," she says. "Though every now and then you have to go to an awards show in the States because there are 60 million people watching."

In the end, although it appeared her publicity was manipulated, especially in Canada, to keep the very audience on which her career depended from knowing her too well, it appeared the Canadian public appreciated that fact, even if they didn't understand her as well as they might have. Articles about Murray focused on those views which Canadians apparently hold dear. Canadian Press writer Stephen Nicholls, for example, noting that Canadians seem to hold a special attachment to her and singer-songwriter Gordon Lightfoot, portrayed Murray as a Canadian family woman first and a career person second.

"I think the reason for that was we always lived here,' Murray said about herself and Lightfoot. "We didn't choose to live any-where else. You know what Canadians are like. If you stay at home and live here, they think that's ever so good, you know."

Nicholls said this view by her Canadian audience suits Murray just fine because she relishes the home life. Nicholls not only repeated that she and Bill Langstroth are raising two kids but stressed that this is her first priority.

"I tour the minimum amount. I have a band on retainer and I have an office to run, so I have to keep the wheels turning. I have to tour a certain amount of the year. Also, it keeps the tools tuned," said Murray. "I do between 70 and 80 dates a year, which is not an awful lot. But it's plenty for me. We're trying to raise a family. I have to be real careful that I'm here a lot. When you're younger it doesn't seem to matter as much. You're just going all the time. I got tired of it and soon I had to get some rhyme and reason to the way it was being done. You do what you have to do and you make sure your priorities are straight. I had the family and just tried to work the career around it. It's strange how those things happen. My career was at its highest peak to date when I was pregnant with my second child and had a baby at home."

While Balmur approved of stories such as these, there were others which demonstrated that Murray was intent on main-taining her career. It was apparent, although Murray had put herself in control of her own career and was intent on balancing it with her home life, she was nonetheless eager to focus on the professional side of her life and the maintenance of her superstar status. In fact, as Chris Dafoe wrote in *The Globe & Mail*, even the impending opening of the Anne Murray Centre in Springhill was occasion to sternly remind everyone that neither she nor her career were dead yet.

"The computer printout, hot off the wire from Nashville, must be at least two and a half metres long. Unfurled it reaches from floor to ceiling, a list of every song that Anne Murray has ever recorded in her twenty years with Capitol Records, from *Snowbird* to *Slow Passing Time*," reported Dafoe.

"Oh, that's wonderful," says Murray's publicist as the list is held aloft. "Why don't we get a couple of copies and have them museum-mounted?"

"Suddenly, Murray, who has been laughing, looks very cross," wrote Dafoe.

"Now look, I warned you guys not to bring up that museum stuff."

Dafoe explained that the word Murray used wasn't "stuff." And although he reported she was kidding, he added "she *is* a little sensitive about all this 'museum' talk. This summer, a building holding a collection of Murray memorabilia will open in Springhill, N.S., the small mining town where the singer was born and raised. It will be called the Anne Murray Centre. It will not be called the Anne Murray Museum."

Dafoe reported that Murray was, at 43 years of age at the time, healthy, relaxed, and content. He also reported that the Anne Murray Centre was essentially Murray's own idea, although Leonard Rambeau once took credit and so, indeed, has Springhill itself.

"I emptied my house into this place," said Murray. "I know it's not a very Canadian thing to do. I got the idea when I was down in Nashville — everyone's got their own museum down there. But the town wanted something and the province wanted something and yes, my basement was getting far too crowded. Seriously though, I hope it will be a shot in the arm for Springhill. But we *don't* call it a museum. I'm not dead yet."

From there, Dafoe, stalking an elusive Anne Murray for some tidbits about what she's really like, settled on the fact that she enjoys sports such as tennis, walking, and swimming, noting as well that she had recently quit smoking, characteristics deemed a further indication that the Anne Murray Centre is not a museum, that its namesake is as healthy as you can get. "And after more than two decades, Murray's career isn't in bad shape either. While her last album, AS I AM, didn't sell as well as she expected, Murray maintains a rapport with her audience that makes it likely that her Toronto stand [five nights at the O'Keefe Centre] will sell out. Her latest effort, a duet with Kenny Rogers, will be included in a greatest-hits package to be released in the fall. And then there's Balmur . . . As well as handling Murray's affairs, the company manages George Fox, one of Canada's most promising country singers.

It is also rumored to be looking into buying the Toronto Maple Leafs. (Murray says she's leaving that to her business manager, although she says she's a rabid hockey fan and admits she's disappointed 'that Toronto doesn't have a real hockey team.')"

Hockey, as has already been noted, is a passion of Murray's. Not only is it included in her on-stage banter in such remote "hockey" territories as Las Vegas, but Elspeth Cameron reported as well, commenting on Murray's intelligence in many areas, "Or ask the Balmur staff. Guess who usually wins the hockey pool?" Sports, especially golf, have been a keen interest of Murray since here childhood. The Anne Murray Centre includes several displays of sporting equipment from her youth. Murray's commitment to aligning the demands of her career with those of her private life include an attention to sporting activities. In fact, she has been one of the celebrities in the pro-am section of the Colgate Dinah Shore Golf Tournament in Palm Springs, California. As the story goes, a year earlier in Lake Tahoe where she was doing a Bing Crosby special, she, Billy Jean King, and pro golfer Sandra Palmer hit a few balls on the practice range. According to reports, King and Palmer admired her swing and suggested she should be in the celebrity section of the Dinah Shore tournament. Although she did not take it seriously at the time, she had no choice when an official invitation arrived and she decided to accept it. It was a family affair. Husband Bill Langstroth drove her cart and acted as her caddy. In the end, she did not attract much of a gallery, with the likes of Bob Hope, Bing Crosby, Jack Lemmon, Dinah Shore and various top women pros on hand, but she did turn in a 99 and her team shot 9 under par.

Other writers have discerned that Murray is fiercely competitive and have likened her drive to win in sports to the mysterious element in her character which drives her in her career. Elspeth Cameron, for instance, related her interest in athletics to her need to be in control. "Out of this athletically thin, cool blonde still pours a voice that is fat and dark, rich and sensual. A voice that recalls a strong earth mother who has never lost sight of the gamey vulgar kid in herself," wrote Cameron. "Today, Anne Murray is right where she wants to be: in control."

"It's only in the last three years that I've felt comfortable onstage," admitted Murray who once swore she would sing only until she made enough money to retire.

"Now, ironically, she finds working fun," said Cameron. "Compared with the old days when her band might get stoned or drunk, or the stage lights might fail, there's enough money to pay for the best players, the best equipment." As Murray put it, "One of the greatest things is being able to walk onstage and not worry about anything except what *I* have to do."

Said Cameron, "The way Anne Murray figures it, she's still pretty outrageous. 'Well, not publicly, maybe, but personally.' When she gets uptight about career pressures, she can always say, 'Well, piss on that,' and go play golf. Come to think of it, it wasn't so long ago that she got ticked off for wearing short shorts at the Thornhill Country Club. Kind of reminds you of her first Las Vegas appearance way back in 1971, when she got told not to wear hot pants and go barefoot onstage."

The search for the real Anne Murray continued — jock, entertainer, loving mother, rebel in hot pants. Chris Dafoe reported that Murray prefers the discipline of the studio to the unpredictability of live performance, was one kind of person professionally and another when she was at home. "That's my work," said Murray. "I do it well. But I'm a real Gemini. I'm completely different at home than when I'm on tour. You have to be real sharp when you're touring — I'm dull normal at home — so when I come off the road, my kids have to put up with Mom making cracks every five minutes for a couple of days. But after that, I totally turn it off and forget what I do for a living until it's time to go out again."

During the 1980s, this kind of analysis of Murray seemed to preoccupy us. Even interviewers and writers from the Maritimes ran into that elusive mix of public and private, lost on the one hand in the achievements, lost further on the other by Murray's stubborn insistence that she was a private person in a public forum.

When Murray was profiled near the end of the 1980s in her home-province newspaper, the *Chronicle-Herald* in Halifax, it was necessary to review some of her accomplishments, as if to overstate the complexity of the woman's public and private life. A more private Anne Murray seemed to emerge, but all that was really available for digestion were the heights to which her star had sailed in the heavens of popular music, an ascendency Murray is convinced Canadians do not understand.

"When Anne Murray's Springhill classmates prophesied in their high school yearbook that she'd become a big star, everyone laughed because it was so unbelievable," wrote Beth Gorham. "No one's laughing now."

Demonstrating both sides of Murray's life by mentioning that Murray was on the day of the interview "in the thick of juggling home, children and business, as her eight-year-old daughter, Dawn, ran around the house shrieking," Gorham presented the career successes as well, not to mention Murray's surprise that Canadians understood her successes least of all. "Murray has sold more albums than almost any female recording artist in the world, with the exception of such luminaries as Barbra Streisand, Linda Ronstadt and Donna Summer. Bruce Springsteen opened for her in 1975. Kenny Rogers was once her lead-in act. So was Billy Joel, more than once.

"Still, 'I think Canadians sometimes fail to realize what an impact I have had in the business,' Murray said in an interview from her Thornhill, Ont., home. "You know it's funny that I should say that because I've never really said it before, but I get more respect in the United States than I do here.' "

According to Gorham, Murray was still torn by the struggle between being a "supermom" and a superstar. "I feel guilty even here now. In another fifteen minutes I've got to start getting ready to do a show. I've seen my kids for half an hour this morning and it'll be fifteen minutes, half an hour tonight and then off I go. You shouldn't feel guilty, but you can't help it. It's important that they know I'm independent . . . I have to maintain my own identity. I think that's good for them to see."

According to Gorham, Murray's brother, Bruce, retired from the music business and living in Oakville, Ontario, explained, "She's been able — it's a cliche, but — to stop and smell the roses along the way and experience her kids and be able to golf and do all the things she does and not have to be frantic about it. She has chosen not to make as much money. Her agents would say, well, if you come back the first of August instead of coming back the middle of August, you can make a couple more million dollars at the state fairs. It's a bone of contention in Hollywood with her. She says, 'Well, so what?' It doesn't make you any happier and she's got two more weeks with her kids."

Murray, by this time, reported Gorham, was taking her fame and accomplishments in stride. "I take it for granted now," said Murray. "That's the way my life is. I finally decided this is what I'm doing for a living. You know, after seventeen, eighteen years, it's been socked home — this is what I do, this is who you are and you must act accordingly, you're a grown-up now. I forget about fame a lot you know, and then I go, 'Oh dear, that's right.'

"It's easier now because I don't have anything to prove anymore. I mean I'm doing this tour, but it's like water off a duck's back, quite frankly . . . I don't have to worry about anything except what I have to do. I have such good people around me. Knowing that and walking out on stage really gives you a lot of confidence and you can't help but put on a good show, you know? Feeling those things and that kind of security — it's taken a lot of years. I mean it didn't happen overnight. It's there now and I don't have to push and I'm relaxed with the whole thing. I'm enjoying performing. It's really very comfortable, very nice."

Gorham detected an approachable tendency in Murray that she felt might explain why she was taken for granted in Canada, that her achievements were not readily understood. She suggested that Murray was too down-to-earth to be readily thought of as the "premier songstress in the world of music," and cited this anecdote told by Murray:

"My daughter caught me in bed at seven o'clock yesterday," said Murray. "and I was sort of snapping — well, I crack my knuckles — and she said, 'You know what you should do onstage, you should crack your knuckles and gross the audience right out.' "

Perhaps the most revealing yet enigmatic portrait of Murray is one written in 1993 by Judy Steed in *The Toronto Star*. The article is revealing because it frankly refers to the tendency of Murray's management to keep her concealed from her audience, unless, of course, it suits their purposes. It is apparent, as well, that this direction is not initiated by management but implemented by management as part of Murray's own requirements. Writer Larry LeBlanc refers to her image as air-brushed. The need to present this elusive portrait to her fans may very well come from Murray herself. It may be that Murray wishes to exercise that control over her life she seems to require, the control which sustains the career while ensuring that the need to succeed is moderated by more human qualities. Often, however, the result has been an elusive distance.

As Steed reported, "In Vegas, she warbles *You Needed Me* . . . the audience of middle-aged Americans melts in their seats, mouthing the words in a rapturous swoon. Many of them have seen her on her endless road trips; at 47, she still travels 80 to 100 days a year, the minimum required to maintain visibility and get the best bookings, hauling with her two 18-wheelers and a crew of 22, including musicians. . . . In real life, she's a jock — the only major ambition she's ever revealed, apart from her work, was her desire to buy Maple Leaf Gardens (Harold Ballard turned her down). She golfs, swims five days a week in the indoor pool at home in Thornhill, cross-country skis in winter. Murray likes to remark on what good shape she's in, and she is — apart from that pesky back. She has scoliosis (curvature of the spine) and two neat surgical incisions on each knee."

As Steed noted, "Balmur occupies swank offices on the top floor of a North York highrise that looks straight down Yonge Street to Lake Ontario. The entrance is always locked, protected by surveillance cameras; the security surrounding Murray is tight. She can never go anywhere alone; kooks are attracted to celebrities, and Murray's had her share, including the Saskatchewan farmer who's pursued her for decades. He's no joke. At one concert, she reached down to accept a bouquet of flowers and it was him; he grabbed her hands and wouldn't let go. She guards her private life. Talk about setting boundaries: never in all my years in journalism have I been so carefully controlled. Not that she's an ogre: she's super-friendly and tons of fun, but make no mistake, she's in charge, and not in a demure way. This is a female peacock who loves to strut her stuff. To use her own term of endearment for women, she's 'a great broad.' She's also a historic figure: as Ben Mink, musical partner of k.d. lang puts it, 'Anne started out barefoot on stage and she's paved the way for the rest of us. She's the first international star out of Canada who kept her Canadian base.' "

Steed's story makes much of Murray's need for a private life presenting itself as a wall, often in the form of Leonard Rambeau.

"You have to keep a sense of distance (from the public)," Rambeau said. "You should say no as much as you say yes." Reported Steed, "To *The Star's* request he responded with a friendly negative: no interview with Murray; no pictures — not until autumn, when she releases her new album . . . . *The Star* decided to go ahead with the story, and three days before my scheduled arrival in Vegas, Rambeau decided 'reluctantly' to co-operate. He doesn't like reporters wandering about unaccompanied. The pristine image is maintained with scrupulous care," wrote Steed.

Not only does Murray's attempt to maintain privacy and perhaps manipulate what information is eventually served to an adoring public demonstrate control, it also seems to reflect a mixed feeling she has about the ambition which ultimately made her successful, the forum in which she achieved her success, and her need to appear to be just like an ordinary person. Or is that too, simply just image? Some of this ambivalence — about whether pursuing success is somehow a little tacky — is revealed in her sentiments about Las Vegas, despite the economic prosperity Las Vegas has brought to her. She recalled for Steed, "I've been through the two shows a night routine, off at two a.m., babies up at six a.m. From '80 to '84, I was here [in Vegas] for 52 weeks, the kids grew up here, this was a way to be in one place and make a lot of money. I was at the peak of my career. Vegas served my purposes well, but it doesn't mean you have to like it. Even after all these years, I still come here and I think, 'God, what is it?' "

Even in 1993, Murray was still attributing much of her success to that turning point in her life when she gave birth for the first time. According to Steed, when Murray was asked when she got "the big vision, the grand ambition," she did not admit it was as a youngster. Instead, she talks about the birth of her first child as "the turning point." She'd longed to have children, became pregnant in 1975, was on the road until she was seven months pregnant, demanding pizzas with pineapple at two a.m.

"When William was born, I thought, wow, if I can do that, I can do anything. I felt like I was the first woman in the world who'd ever given birth," Murray told Steed. William, it is reported, was born as musical as his parents, began to play the drums at four and, that summer, going on seventeen, played at the Halifax jazz festival with Georges Hebert. "William's dedicated," his mom said. "He knows more about music than I do."

There were also reports at the time that daughter Dawn, going on fourteen, also had a great singing voice. Langstroth said then that their kids can hardly escape the music business. "It's in their genes."

Murray's image of herself is that she has somehow kept the component of her personality which was native to Springhill, the down home girl-next-door, from being obfuscated by her drive to achieve success in a business where performers fall victim to their own legends quite frequently. Reminded frequently that she was the favorite female singer of Elvis Presley, Murray uses the subject to underline her search for privacy, her resolve to delineate between show business and the real person she, at the same time, wishes to be. Elvis, she said, fell prey to the music business.

"He was a victim. He was manipulated. That could never happen to me," Murray told Steed.

Steed homed in on the conflicts which can arise, how one of the highlights of her career was marred by the news of a death of a friend, and how she had to carry on anyway. "Something she loved: being asked to sing the national anthem before the first World Series game in Canada when the Blue Jays played the Atlanta Braves," wrote Steed. "Except: 'I was getting ready to go down there (to SkyDome) and I got a phone call; my oldest friend died. It was a big shock, she was a singer from *Singalong Jubilee*, she was a great broad and I miss her.' It's hard to make friends in showbiz, she says. 'You always think there are ulterior motives.' "

In her private life, by most reports, Murray is competitive and she puts the same drive into her private life that is required to sustain such a long career. "She grabs her racquet," wrote Steed, "and joins selected band members, plus the aforementioned tennis pro, on the courts. She's fiercely competitive, hits hard, too hard — hence the back injury."

But what about friendship? Can a woman juggling two priorities, career and family, a woman with a definite idea that she does not want to fall victim to the business in which she earns a successful living, find the kind of friendship many of us take for granted? Steed talked to a neighbor in Thornhill to try to get the answer to that question. " 'Anne was living like a hermit,' says Cynthia McReynolds, describing their early encounters in Thornhill. McReynolds, who looks like the older sister Murray never had, has a tennis court in her backyard and invited the famous neighbor to use it. Making friends with Cynthia 'was like being saved,' Murray says. McReynolds has a circle of women friends who provided a connection into neighborhood life which Murray treasures."

Much has been written over the years about other superstar performers who feel isolated by their profession. Murray, however, seems aware there is a price to pay on the one hand, yet on the other considers her career, no matter how important, a secondary part of her personality. "Whatever happens to Murray, however, she has come to one over-riding conclusion," wrote another *Toronto Star* writer, Bruce Blackadar a few years before Steed. "I've had a really good career, but quite frankly I'd rather be a well-rounded human being than a well rounded performer . . . One thing I've always had is common sense, and a lot of people have found it boring.

"But it's kept me alive."

Anne is flanked by two Royal Canadian Mounted Policemen at a press reception.

With her manager Leonard Rambeau following her, Anne Murray greets various civic dignitaries on the reception line formed at the opening of the Anne Murray Centre.

Released in 1980, ANNE MURRAY'S GREATEST HITS *sold over 6 million copies before* VOLUME II *was released in 1989.*

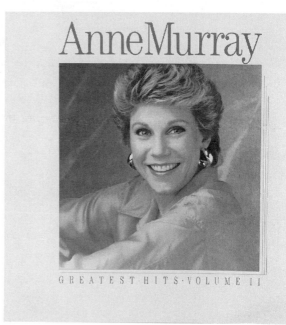

CHAPTER ELEVEN

Time Don't Run Out On Me

I feel I have a knack for picking the right songs. Lord knows I spend enough time listening to demos and material that is submitted to us.
— Anne Murray

In the period between what some have considered the peak of Anne Murray's career, at the end of the 1970s with the tremendous success of *You Needed Me*, and now, Murray has herself staunchly used terms such as "career to date" to describe her life as an artist. The woman who once was so ambivalent about a career in the music business is steadfastly aware that she has no intention of retiring, nor should she at this time, only 50 years old. But if at one time it had appeared to some that her arrival on the edifice of superstardom was a matter of pure chance, by the time Anne Murray rolled into the 1990s, it became apparent she had achieved such a status because she had every intention of doing so, right from the beginning. By the end of the 1980s and well into this decade, Murray began to make the adjustment required by technological and economic developments in the music business. And while record sales had a tendency to diminish, especially in comparison to her peak in the late 1970s, her position as superstar nonetheless remained entrenched. Anne Murray was now an institution in Canada, but it was clear, as she herself had said, that she wasn't dead yet.

And with respect to achievements and accolades, the question remains whether the end of the 1970s was really her peak. A variety of facts would bear out that she had been right all along, with regard to her ambition to have a long career, that the tributes, honors, and success would continue through the 1980s well into the 1990s. A look at her recordings, her live performances, and her new musical initiatives after her so-called peak period shows that she was willing to break new ground and keep her career vital and focused. Bearing this out, a new album is anticipated in 1996, complete with studio duets with Bryan Adams and Aaron Neville.

As reporter Tom McCoag in the Amherst Bureau of Halifax's *Chronicle-Herald* points out in a 1991 snippet (Amherst is a half hour drive from Springhill at most), "Springhill native and international singing star Anne Murray has been one of the world's most popular entertainers for more than twenty years. Her track record is astonishing. She has scored an impressive array of hits on the country, pop, and adult contemporary charts since her first smash hit *Snowbird* in 1970. The recording was so successful, Ms. Murray became the first Canadian female solo artist to be awarded a U.S. gold record. The hits continued and she has garnered eleven U.S. gold and multi-platinum records, three Country Music Association Awards, four American Music Awards, four Grammy Awards, more than twenty Juno Awards and numerous industry awards."

Indeed, throughout the 1980s and into the 1990s, she has continued to rack up successes. Some specific highlights include the celebration of Anne Murray Week in Los Angeles in 1980, a year which also saw the release of her first *Greatest Hits* album which would go on to sell six million copies worldwide. That same year, she took home her Grammy for the song *Could I Have This Dance.* As the rest of the decade unfolded, a 1982 Christmas special was watched by 3 million viewers in Canada (over 10 percent of the population) and a further 24 million in the United States (almost 10 percent of the population). Then, in 1983, she gathered up the Grammy for the song *A Little Good News* which, it was reported, was a favorite song of then U.S. Vice President George Bush. In 1985, Murray was awarded the Order of Canada, the same year the Anne Murray Centre was proposed for Springhill. By the time the Centre's sod had been turned in 1986 and officially opened in 1989, she had continued on with a critically acclaimed television special, *Anne Murray in Disney World.*

Any questions about the impact of her private life on her productivity during this same period can be answered by the tremendous amount of recording she accomplished. Her output during the 1980s and early 1990s was astonishing: A COUNTRY COLLECTION, SOMEBODY'S WAITING, and GREATEST HITS in 1980; WHERE DO YOU GO WHEN YOU DREAM? and CHRISTMAS WISHES in 1981; HOTTEST NIGHT OF THE YEAR (1982), A LITTLE GOOD NEWS (1983), HEART OVER MIND (1984), SOMETHING TO TALK ABOUT (1986), HARMONY and ANNE MURRAY'S COUNTRY HITS (1987), AS I AM and CHRISTMAS (1988), and GREATEST HITS VOLUME II (1989). And in this decade, among her releases have been YOU WILL (1990), YES I DO (1991), FIFTEEN OF THE BEST (1992), and a long-awaited and long-planned tribute to the songs and singers of the 1940s and 50s, CROONIN' in 1993. CROONIN' is among her bestsellers and provided listeners with what could be the best voice in modern popular music interpreting songs which have been cherished for half a century.

It wasn't until YES I DO that Murray performed in French. *If Ever I See You Again* was sung in English and French. "I'm just ashamed that I haven't done something in French sooner," said Murray, according to reporter Steve Nicholls. She had studied French at university, but hired a tutor to help her through the translated lyrics. "No, she says, the song wasn't planned to coincide with Canada's unity debate, but she does feel 'we have to find a way to keep Quebec within the country and stay the way we are . . . We aren't a complete country without Quebec.' "

But Murray remains noted for her recording professionalism rather than the political thrust of her music. As Perry Stern noted in his article in *Canadian Musician*, "Once in the studio, Anne is truly in her element."

"The best part of it is getting together with the musicians when they haven't heard the songs yet," said Murray. "We play the demo for them just to give them the idea, then I walk into the booth. I start to sing and they start to play. I have to know the song really well before I go to the studio. Kyle [Lehning] was blown away because he's never known anybody who's been that prepared. I feel from my very first performance I have to get the musicians excited about what they're doing. I learned that very early on."

As Peter Stern observes, "The professionalism that Anne exerts in the studio, and demands of those who work around her, ultimately comes out in the mix. That she is plainly a thinking, caring individual is translated miraculously onto tape, and that is probably the secret of her unique success."

Added Beaton and Peterson in *Maritime Music Greats*: "Murray's pickiness about the songs she will and won't sing is legendary. Since she doesn't write her own material, she depends on other people to produce songs that fit her voice and personality, and after years of constant use, her intuition is razor-sharp."

"I feel I have a knack for picking the right song. Lord knows I spend enough time listening to demos and material that is submitted to us," she told *Country Music News*. In fact, Murray is reputed to consider hundreds of songs before recording and, in the early days during her association with Brian Ahern, a pool table was quite literally littered with tapes and song proposals. Nonetheless, she has frankly admitted that she makes her mind up quickly and rejected songs enter their state of rejection often with elaborate enthusiasm. At one point she described 90 percent of the material submitted to her as just not worth listening to. Still, the process goes on. Perry Stern recounted that an unnamed tune on her LP *As I Am* was able to overcome Murray's initial disapproval. After it was submitted three times, it was finally accepted for recording.

With regard to the politics of recording, however, there have been serious bumps in the relationship in the more than quarter-century since Murray has been recording. On a number of occasions, Capitol Records and Murray have had disputes over which singles to release and which direction her career should go. Harking back to the early days, Murray's failure to convince Capitol to release her version of Gene MacLellan's *Put Your Hand In The Hand* cost them both another hit record. As well, it was Murray who insisted the smash hit *You Needed Me* should be released as a single. And then there was the high-handed approach taken by Capitol where Tom Catalano was concerned, in the days before Jim Ed Norman came on board. Phil Roura of the *New York Daily News* reported a more serious rift in May of 1992. "The marriage is over. After twenty-two years with Capitol Records, which produced her first hit *Snowbird* in 1970, Anne Murray is getting a divorce."

" 'I'm not going to re-sign with them,' she said from her home in Toronto. 'It's time to call it a day.' "

Roura reported that Murray claimed the split was purely financial but when she was pressed, admitted that the gulf ran deeper than that. " 'They don't want me to do this and they don't want me to do that,' she sighed. 'They want to go with new artists. They have Garth Brooks, who is making them a whole lot of money, and maybe they just don't need me.' "

But Murray said the split wasn't painful. "Not at all,' she quickly stated. "It's simply time to move on. I want to be with a company that thinks of me as more than just a country singer. I have lived under this for years."

"And there's the rub," wrote Roura. "Although embraced by country lovers as one of their own, Murray has never thought of herself as simply a 'country singer.' Indeed, her new album *Yes I Do* — her last for Capitol— contains cuts that defy labels.

" 'I've always thought of myself as a singer — not a person who sings a particular kind of music,' said Murray. 'For years, I was regarded as the queen of middle of the road.' "

Nevertheless, in the end, Murray returned to Capitol (as EMI) in time for *Croonin'*.

But it wasn't only in the area of recorded music that Murray enjoyed an astounding success throughout the last decade and a half. Television specials, including numerous guest slots with a variety of entertainers, but especially those in which she was the host, have drawn staggeringly high numbers of viewers. Her 1988 Christmas special, for example, turned out to be the number one rated showed on the English CBC network that year and the highest-rated variety show for more than a decade.

"The ratings came out and I got a phone call (from CBC)," Anne Murray was quoted as saying by Stephen Nichols of the Canadian Press. 'When are we going to do the next one?'" The next one, as it turned out, was a special which coincided with the release of her *Anne Murray's Greatest Hits Vol. II*. The show incorporated such hit songs as *You Needed Me, A Little Good News, Now And Forever,* and *Time Don't Run Out On Me*, as well as duets with Kenny Rogers on *If I Ever Fall In Love Again* and with Dave Loggins (Kenny's cousin) on *Nobody Loves Me Like You Do*, as well as several numbers with K.T. Oslin. Coincidentally, the special gave viewers a look at what was then a new Anne Murray Centre in Springhill.

Since then Murray has amassed a long list of highly-rated specials up to and including her Christmas special in 1995. At the same time, she has steadfastly refused to commit herself to a regular television show, apparently fearing the overexposure of television as it pertains to the demand for live appearances, not to mention how such a rigorous schedule would affect her life with her children.

Her specials have had a tendency to reflect a wide variety of musical genres. Often cited as an example are her television specials in general and the *Anne Murray in Disney World* special in particular in which Murray joins a variety of guests and a group of children to explore the tourist attraction. The guests included comedienne Andrea Martin, singer Julio Iglesias, and rocker Patti Labelle, not to mention fellow Canadian singer and songwriter Paul Janz. Her duet with Janz included a full gospel choir. As Beaton and Peterson in *Maritime Music Greats* note, "Since she is a highly intelligent woman with a keen sense of changing trends in the musical marketplace, she sometimes decides to touch all the bases — country, pop, rock and inspirational."

On stage, Murray demonstrates the same professionalism and cool assurance she brings to the recording studio and television special. But sometimes reviews focus on a concern about the recurring ambivalence Murray demonstrates about musical genre. Murray continues undaunted. She has known for many years that a pop music singer has a much longer career in store for her than the average rock singer, many of whom come and go quickly. A review of a Murray concert in 1987 by Chris Dafoe of *The Globe and Mail* reveals a flavor of confusion about what Murray musically intends even while her live presentation clears up any misgivings about the quality of her voice and performance. "Anne Murray has been 'Canada's Songbird' for 17 years. And like anything that's been kept in a cage for that long, albeit a gilded one, she occasionally shows some strain," he wrote. "In recent encounters with the press, Murray has bridled at the persistence of the image of the fresh-scrubbed young girl from Nova Scotia, and her fans' concern with the trivialities of her image: her new hairstyle, her 'daring' dresses.

"And her records, like those of most pop musicians — middle of the road, or otherwise — do little to betray her status as 'national treasure.' Annie may be a Canadian monument, but on vinyl it doesn't show.

"But when she performs live, as she did last night at the O'Keefe Centre, all the frustrations of the *Songbird* status are turned to gentle jibes, and the Canadianarama — jokes about Lethbridge, fond memories of the Maritimes — comes out in spades. But so does the voice, a strong, superbly controlled instrument that seems to have ripened and grown more versatile with time. It is impressive even when it delivers some of the white-bread banalities that have been hits for Murray over the last seventeen years. That voice

SNOWBIRD: THE STORY OF ANNE MURRAY

makes all the talk about Anne's new hemline or Anne's new coiffure (and sometimes, unfortunately, some of Anne's songs) seem irrelevant.

"Murray opened her two-hour show with a set leaning heavily toward ballads and older, more familiar material — *Danny's Song, I Just Fall In Love Again, Shadows In The Moonlight* — while gently jibing the audience about its preconceptions about what an Anne Murray should be like and herself about the Anne Murray she was presenting. She carried it off with a good deal of charm and more than a little bawdy humor."

Dafoe recounted the audience's dismay when Murray emerged in black tights and a gold lamé jerkin, strutting to a throbbing synthesizer beat of *Heartaches*, and he commented, "As shocking as this shouldn't be (this *is* 1987; Anne Murray *is* a pop singer) there was a slight, but audible gasp from some quarters." Dafoe added, "Murray's show is a tightly paced, good-humored entertainment, albeit one that takes few chances, and rarely steps out of line by accident. At 40 (a fact she repeatedly and unnecessarily brings up — how old is Mick Jagger?) Murray is a gifted professional, not a teenaged songbird. Thankfully, after last night's show, the cage door seems to be opening."

Murray has also reportedly shown a gift for spontaneous humor, especially in live performance where the various surprises cannot be erased in any other way. During an interview with Peter Gzowski on *Morningside*, she reported an incident at a concert in Grand Rapids, during which her pants had fallen down onstage. Apparently she hiked them up, telling her audience that she had not played Grand Rapids before and was simply trying to make a good impression.

Beaton and Peterson also reported that Murray was virtually perfect in a live concert in Halifax in 1991. Again with corporate sponsorship, this time from IGA, Murray was touring the Maritimes, and concerts included Sydney, Saint John, Charlottetown, and Moncton. "The Halifax concert in early June turned out to be more than two hours of tight, high-energy entertainment. Both musically and technically, there was never a glitch, a miscue or even a hesitation," they wrote in *Maritime Music Greats*.

"Quick to put down any pretensions about her own grandeur,

Murray cracked, 'If there are any songs you don't recognize, they're from my latest album.' She was quick to notice any lull in the applause, and to cut smoothly from patter back to singing. Hit song followed hit song; *I Just Fall In Love Again*, then *I Still Wish The Very Best For You*. Since she was back in her home province, Murray traded on the background and history she shared with the audience, telling them how naive she was as a girl fresh from Nova Scotia, thinking she only had to record the songs she liked, and failing to take account of the difficulty recording stores had in classifying her style. To prove how confusing categories can be, Murray introduced a medley of songs, some of which she had recorded as pop songs and some as middle of the road, but all of which showed up at the top of the country charts. Murray did only a verse or two plus a chorus of each song: *Love Song, Another Sleepless Night, Walk Right Back, He Thinks I Still Care, Just Another Woman In Love*, and *Daydream Believer*. There are probably only a handful of artists besides Murray who could program an entire concert with nothing but number-one hits."

But if there is a restlessness on the part of music pundits about Anne Murray because she is not known as an innovator, there can be little argument about her success, whether Canadians understand it or not, whether they are aware or not of her impact on pop music well beyond our borders, in a world which has taken her as their own musical star. And pushing towards 30 years of musical stardom, she continues to seek out pop hits and combinations which will keep her near the top of the game. The duets with superstar Bryan Adams (himself showing a remarkable longevity) and Aaron Neville, the current flavor of the month, are an indication that Murray by no means intends to retire from a career that has brought her so much success, that has, in truth, realized a dream she had when she was just a youngster.

But Anne Murray is Canadian and herein lies some of the confusion about just who she really is. She has staunchly remained a Canadian, yet repelled the Canadian audience's ownership of her image. And she has lamented that Canadians do not recognize the impact she has made on the world music industry. Perhaps. When we seek acknowledgment, we often seek it at home, right in our own back yards as if this, more than anything else, will verify somehow that we have done the right thing. Yes, Anne Murray is Canadian.

Perry Stern once questioned "What do the Mounties, beavers, hockey players and Anne Murray have in common besides cold winters? They are our cultural icons. They are representative symbols of a nation of outposts strung across a thin line from sea to, well, you know. The RCMP may not always get their man, hockey players might forsake their fans and move to L.A., [there's a photograph of Murray with Wayne Gretzky prominently displayed in the Anne Murray Centre] beavers are rodents who live partly under water with flat tails and terrible overbites, but Anne Murray, Our Anne, never waivers.

"And the best thing about Our Anne, The Springhill Songbird, besides, of course, the music she's shared with us over the past twenty years (forgetting the rest of the world for the moment, as we Canadians are wont to do), is that she couldn't give two hoots about iconography.

"Not a tinker's dam.

"And do you know why? Simple. Because she knows, unlike us, that it's all an illusion. We may think Anne's been here forever, but she knows about the ups and downs. We may think Anne's still the down east barefoot tomboy, singing about banks, singing about cars, singing about Canada; but Anne knows that she is a mother first, a wife second, and that only one other woman in history [Barbra Streisand] has sold more albums than she has. And that's another reason why she fits so well as a Canadian icon. That's right. We're Number Two!"

But it's more than Stern's rather droll observation about Canadian icons. It's that a young woman from the Maritimes in general and Springhill in particular, even on the world stage, is going to make sure she does it right. You can't escape the Maritime tradition and you can't escape how things are supposed to be done. "Nova Scotia has sent hundreds of its sons and daughters down to the road to success, but none has achieved the universal appeal and popularity of Springhill's Anne Murray — no one has remained as true to her roots as Anne Murray," Roland J. Thornhill, Nova Scotia provincial Minister of Tourism said in 1989 at the official opening of the Anne Murray Centre. "The Anne Murray

Centre is not just a museum of artifacts reflecting past glories of a forgotten personality. It is a glowing tribute to a life and career to someone who still calls Nova Scotia home."

According to the Springhill and Parrsboro *Record*, Thornhill said the career of Springhill's songbird reflected the truths and values that Nova Scotians hold dear, and was a fine example of these values in action. "A belief in the sanctity of the family, of respect for home and community, a belief that hard work and dedication can bring success and satisfaction, and a belief that no matter how far you go, you never forget where you've come from," the Minister concluded. "Anne Murray has never forgotten. Now, with the completion of this centre, Springhill has returned the favor."

But, in Nashville, every musical star has a center or equivalent. So that a person gets to wondering. How does a reluctant singer with one of the finest pop voices ever overcome her fears and become Anne Murray, all the while making sure the world doesn't get to know her? What puts in place that apparent need for the contrast between public and private? Or are we simply looking at the rewards and penalties of manipulation? Leonard Rambeau's comment that an Anne Murray has to say no as often as she says yes. Rewards and penalties. By the time Anne Murray changed her mind from no to yes on an anthology recording dedicated to breast cancer research and development, there wasn't room for her to appear with myriad of stars who had more quickly said yes.

And wondering about questions like that, one remembers Springhill, Nova Scotia, how far removed it is from where Anne Murray is now, but how she still returns there to remember her roots and apply them to a larger world stage. In this way, despite her ambition to be a star, she remains human and approachable, the kind of inspiration which inevitably results in an unwilling assumption of the status of institution.

If anything has come to an end at this stage in Murray's life and career, it is nothing more than that sense of loss of control she endured in the early days. Now, with so much success behind her and perhaps more ahead of her, she remains in control of her own fate. This certainty, more than anything else, probably was born in Springhill, Nova Scotia.

Images of Anne Murray for the past decade.

AFTERWORD

Two worlds.

At the Anne Murray Centre, this being Christmas, the gift shop is staying open extra hours for the convenience of Christmas shoppers. The gift shop, everyone learns, is located at the completion of the series of video and audio displays and artifacts which cumulatively catalogue Anne Murray's career so far. This decision, in the parlance of the tourism industry, represents good business. Tourists, with dollars in their pockets and that sense of benevolence and star association one gets after touring a complex and impressive display in which someone of humble means reaches musical superstardom, can be readily enticed to look through the goods for sale. Their purchases help offset the costs of operating the Anne Murray Centre.

There is, of course, memorabilia of Murray on hand, cards and other small tokens, stuffed animals, tote bags with the Anne Murray Centre printed on the outside. It's homey for a gift shop, the kind of gift shop where you feel like standing around to have a chat. Or is that just an extension of the personality of Springhill where conversation often breaks out with an unusual warmth and interest, unusual at least by Ontario standards?

Anne Murray, it would appear, is a bridge between two worlds.

The other one, of course, is celebrity like the Juno Awards which, in 1996, Springhill's Anne Murray hosted. Most Canadians have seen shows such as these dozens of times, the Junos and the Grammys and the Emmys and even the Oscars, the audience dressed up in tuxedos or fashionable gowns. We know the glitter and sparkle of it all, the slick television direction, cameras which pan the famous faces, superimposing their names underneath their upper torsos, less to ensure we know who they are, than to build some excitement, some tension.

All award shows reflect an industry's self-indulgence, it's a party which toasts itself, whether such parties are the Junos, the Grammys, or the vacuum cleaner sales department's annual shindig. One of the perks of being part of a group is the opportunity to win peer-acknowledgement for our efforts and our talents. This is especially true up there in the higher rafters of "awardsdom," because we, the fans of our entertainers, have a tendency to treat them like aristocrats, making them in the image of what we would like to be, at least on days when things have been a little tough at the office.

Anne Murray, the bridge between two worlds.

The breakfast club at the Rollways Motel in Springhill, everyone in a padded parka because it's winter, everyone with an opinion and the sense of humor it requires to back it up. The odor of eggs and bacon frying on the grill, administered and nursed along by someone who went to high school with Anne Murray but has her reservations about her friendliness now. And, always, the new arrival coming in, saying, "Hi, Bert," or "Mornin', Fred," then picking on his hat or referring to the dark shadow of beard he hasn't shaved that morning, pouring himself a coffee, then glancing across the dining room to offer even the most casual stranger his refill.

Two worlds.

Las Vegas, neon from bootstraps to pompadour, and Kenny Rogers up there acknowledging Anne Murray in his audience, the same Anne Murray who comes from Springhill where the breakfast club meets. This is just before Rogers receives his gift of a white Stutz-Bearcat, and Murray, whether sincerely or not, murmurs, "I want one of those." George Anthony is right about that. "Springhill was never like this."

Or back on the stage where they're going to hand out the Junos, just for one worrisome cynical second, one hears American singing legend Jim Morrison remarking from the grave: "No one here gets out alive." At first, his remark seems well-placed. He didn't. Janis Joplin didn't. Jimi Hendrix didn't. Elvis didn't. Elvis . . . Murray said that Elvis was manipulated and that she wouldn't let that happen to her, her own association with Elvis' manager, Col. Parker himself, documented, by the way, back in Springhill at the Anne Murray Centre. But she's right. Except, perhaps, for some brief periods with managers who weren't taking her where she wanted to go, that period after *Snowbird* before she married Bill Langstroth, she's entirely right, she hasn't been manipulated, has done it all on her own terms.

In a way, Murray, notwithstanding her sincerity, her dedication to her career, her charm and her unflinching talent, has turned it all around on the audience. In a way, she's manipulated the audience with her deep concern that she avoid being manipulated herself — by demanding a private life and by shielding herself from a public which seems to believe it can expect certain things from her, something in addition to the wonder of her voice.

And sometimes she's gone even further to protect herself and her privacy. She's manipulated her image to keep the career marching ever onwards, suffered the criticisms that have resulted, kept going, not really changing all that much in the end, but coming back to the ingredients of pop music which held a large arena for her and which made her a star. Most of all, she has kept the pristine image of a small-town woman dragged kicking and screaming (but knowing, she has said, from when she was a youngster that she wanted it and could get it) into fame and success. She has kept that image because it was part of her success. And it's kept her alive in a normally unforgiving choice of career.

As Larry LeBlanc wrote twenty-two years ago in his profile of Anne Murray, performers don't get to pick their audiences, it's the other way around. But Anne Murray has labored to pick her audience and, for the most part, it's the same audience which picked her.

Anne Murray is considered by most to be a Canadian icon. She represents all that Canadians hold dear, not in our performing stars necessarily, but in a broader sense, what Canadians perceive to be worthwhile human characteristics. She has maintained her residence in Canada and has dutifully gone home to Nova Scotia for the holidays. She has shown that she was a mother first, a wife second, and a career person third. She comes from relatively humble circumstances and has shown that special gift of drive and single-minded purpose which originates best of all in the Maritimes. This drive and ambition seems as much a gift as that wonderful voice which she characterizes herself as "fat." She has appealed to that Canadian sense, ingrained forever, that hard work pays off, that a person should set sights on a goal and then pursue it. And above all, never forget to acknowledge that place of your youth where all the seeds were sown.

Although Anne Murray is a world star, perhaps the first truly world star Canada has produced, with a career which has blossomed for more than a quarter century and shows no signs of truly abating, she remains our icon because, in a sense, she remains us, Canadians with rather conservative ethics and practices. It's more than remembering your home town, more than attending your high-school reunion no matter how famous you are, more than clinging to the family bonds you've established. In Murray's case, it's even more than bringing it all home to Springhill, the celebration of making it and making it big, as acknowledgement. No, sometimes, this Canadian ethic includes maintaining the image even on those rare occasions when you let some of it briefly slip and something more provocative peeks out from underneath, like the glimpse of a shapely leg.

Canadians get over someone's spiked-hairdo-miniskirt image whims, consider them brief indiscretions. What does it matter as long as the commitment to family, hard work, and your roots, along with a generous amount of financial ambition, still throb in your soul? In the end, Anne Murray is just what most Canadians would be, given the talent and the circumstances.

And, if you are Anne Murray, you can get as annoyed as you want at the possessiveness of your Canadian audience who want to remind you of what your are and how you should remain that way, at Canadians who don't look at the larger world to measure how its partisans are doing *on that level*, at Canadians who — when they see you demonstrating their principles and view of life — take possession of you and won't let go, calling you an institution or an ambassador of their way of life. Doesn't matter if you get annoyed. It's all forgiveable for Canadians.

Which is one of the reasons so many of Anne Murray's songs have infiltrated our consciousness, why so many to come will probably do the same thing. You see, we're all born in a Springhill. No matter how small our accomplishments shrink that larger world around us. This, after all, is Canada. This, you see, is "Anne Murray country."

DISCOGRAPHY

SINGLES

What About Me 1968
Bidin' My Time 1970
Snowbird 1970
Sing Hi, Sing Low 1970
A Stranger In My Place 1971
It Takes Time 1971
Talk It Over In The Morning
   1971
I Say A Little Prayer/By The
   Time I Get To Phoenix
   (with Glen Campbell) 1971
Cotton Jenny 1972
Robbie's Song For Jesus 1972
Danny's Song 1972/73
What About Me 1973
Send A Little Love My Way
   1973
Love Song 1973/74
He Thinks I Still Care 1974
Son Of A Rotten Gambler
   1974
You Won't See Me 1974
Children of My Mind 1974
Just One Look 1974
Day Tripper 1974/75

Uproar   1975
Sunday Sunrise   1975
The Call   1976
Golden Oldie   1976
Things   1976
Sunday School To Broadway   1977
Walk Right Back   1978
You Needed Me   1978
Hey Daddy   1978/79
I Just Fall In Love Again   1979
Shadows In The Moonlight   1979
Broken Hearted Me   1979
Daydream Believer   1979
Why Don't You Stick Around
    1979/80
Lucky Me   1980
I'm Happy Just To Dance With
    You   1980
Could I Have This Dance   1980
Blessed Are The Believers   1981
It's All I Can Do   1981
We Don't Have To Hold
    Out   1981
Another Sleepless Night   1982
Hey! Baby!   1982
Somebody's Always Saying
    Goodbye   1982/83
A Little Good News   1983
That's Not The Way It's
    Supposed To Be   1984
Just Another Woman In Love   1984
Nobody Loves Me Like You Do
    1984
That's Not The Way   1984
I Don't Think I'm Ready For You
    1985

Time Don't Run Out On Me
 1985
Who's Leaving Who   1986
Now and Forever (*You And Me*)   1986
My Life's A Dance   1986
Are You Still In Love With Me
 1987
Anyone Can Do The Heartbreak
 1987
On And On   1987
Perfect Strangers (with DOUG MALLORY)   1988
Flying On Your Own   1988
Slow Passin' Time   1988/89
Who But You   1989
I'll Be Your Eyes   1989
If I Ever Fall In Love Again
(with KENNY ROGERS)   1989
Feed This Fire   1990
Bluebird   1990
Everyday   1991
Si Jamais Je Te Revois   1991
I Can See Arkansas   1992
Are You Still In Love With Me
1992
Make Love To Me   1993
The Wayward Wind   1994
Born To Be With You   1994
Over You   1994/95

DISCOGRAPHY

ALBUMS/CDS

WHAT ABOUT ME   1968
THIS WAY IS MY WAY   1969
SNOWBIRD   1970
HONEY, WHEAT &
   LAUGHTER   1970
STRAIGHT, CLEAN & SIMPLE
   1971
TALK IT OVER IN THE
   MORNING   1971
ANNE MURRAY/GLEN
   CAMPBELL   1971
ANNIE   1972
DANNY'S SONG   1973
LOVE SONG   1974
COUNTRY   1974
HIGHLY PRIZED POSSESSION   1974
TOGETHER   1975
KEEPING IN TOUCH   1976
THERE'S A HIPPO
   IN MY TUB   1977
LET'S KEEP IT THAT WAY   1978
NEW KIND OF FEELING   1979
I'LL ALWAYS LOVE YOU   1979

A COUNTRY COLLECTION 1980
SOMEBODY'S WAITING 1980
GREATEST HITS 1980
SOMETHING TO TALK ABOUT
 1986
HARMONY 1987
ANNE MURRAY'S COUNTRY HIT
 1987
AS I AM 1988
CHRISTMAS 1988
GREATEST HITS VOLUME II
 1989
YOU WILL 1990
YES I DO 1991
FIFTEEN OF THE BEST 1992
CROONIN' 1993
THE BEST . . . SO FAR 1994
NOW AND FOREVER
 (box set) 1994
THE BEST OF THE SEASON
 (reissue of Christmas
 albums) 1994

BIBLIOGRAPHY

Adilman, Sid. "Murray and Rambeau: The Partnership that Works." *Toronto Star*, December 23, 1994.

Anthony, George. "Anne . . . Esthetic.," *Toronto Sun*, July 17, 1977, pp. M5.

Anthony, George. "Anne Murray, 'I Intended To Have a Private Life.'" *Chatelaine*, January, 1975, pp. 28, 80-83.

Anthony, George. "Anne Murray's New Hit, Motherhood." *Chatelaine*, 1976.

Anthony, George. "O'Keefe Snags Anne while She's Hot." *Toronto Star*, 1980.

Anonymous. "Anne Murray Draws Large Crowd at Springhill Re-union Concert." *The Record*, July 27, 1978, p. 1.

Anonymous. "Murray: Rebel with a Cause." *Melody Maker*, April 19, 1975.

Anonymous. Obituary. Springhill and Parrboro *Record*, April 2, 1980, pp. 1.

Beaton, Virginia & Peterson, Stephen. *Maritime Music Greats: Fifty Years of Country and Folk.* Halifax: Nimbus, pp. 111-133, 87-91.

Beaton, Kelly. "AMC Opening Draws Thousands." Springhill and Parrsboro *Record*, Vol. 60. No. 31 (August 2, 1989), p. 1.

Blackadar, Bruce. "Anne's happy on all fronts these days." *Toronto Star*, December 8, 1988, pp. C4.

Cameron, Elspeth. "Anne Murray's Double Life." *Chatelaine*, September, 1988, pp. 115-117, 135-140.

Canadian Press. "Hall of Fame for Anne." *Winnipeg Free Press*, February 4, 1993.

Canadian Press. "Lightfoot, Murray Back Adams' Fight on Content Rules." *Winnipeg Free Press*, January 16, 1992.

Canadian Press. "Murray-Kieling Conflict Becomes Stage-play Topic." *Winnipeg Free Press*, April 7, 1984.

Canadian Press. "Murray Waits for Comeback." *Globe and Mail*, November 19, 1984, pp. M14.

Conlon, Patrick. "Anne Murray's Maritime Mafia." *Toronto Life*, September 1973, pp. 36-39, 74-78.

Dafoe, Chris. "I Think I've Had a Charmed Life." *Globe and Mail*, May 17, 1987.

Dafoe, Chris. "Murray's Timeless Voice Soars Over Frustrations." *Globe and Mail*, May 13, 1987.

Drobot, Eve. "Social & Personal." *Saturday Night*, November, 1989. p. 29.

Dunne, Bob. "Anne Murray, Killing an Image." *Beetle*, 1974.

Flippo, Chet. "Anne Murray's Reluctant Return to the Top." 1978.

Flohil, Richard. "Anne Murray." *Canadian Musician*, 1979.

Fulton, E. Kaye. "The Guy Who Bugs Our Anne." *Toronto Star*, November 3, 1985.

Goddard, Peter. "Anne Murray: A Touch of Class." *Toronto Star*, 1979.

Gorham, Beth. "Murray Finds Harmony with Fame." *Chronicle-Herald*, May 28, 1987.

Howell, Bill. "Upper Canada Romantic." *Maclean's*, May 1972, pp. 29-31, 66-69.

Hunt, Dennis. "Anne Murray — Take Two." *Calendar*, June 22, 1980, pp. 90.

Jackson, Rick. *Encyclopedia of Canadian Rock, Pop & Folk Music*. Kingston: Quarry Press Inc., 1994, pp. 205-207.

King, Paul. "Jackpot." *Today*, 1978.

Lacey, Liam. "I'm Really an Old Rock and Roller at Heart." *Globe and Mail*, April 20, 1985, pp. 7.

LeBlanc, Larry. "The Flip Side of Anne Murray." *Maclean's*, November 1974, pp. 86-91.

Little, Marilee. "A Little Good News." *The Atlantic Advocate*, May, 1989. pp. 8-11.

Livingstone, David. *Anne Murray: The Story So Far*. New York: Madison Press Books, 1981.

McCoag, Tom. "Murray's Path to Stardom Paved with Gold, Platinum." *Chronicle-Herald*, June 5, 1991, pp. B5.

McDonald, Marci. "Zap! And It's a New Anne Murray." *Toronto Star*, November 1973.

Moore, Micki. "The Career Has To Work around the Family." *Toronto Star*, May 15, 1989. pp. C1-C2.

Muretich, James. "Anne's Out to Enjoy Her Success." *Calgary Herald*, April 10, 1987.

Nichols, Stephen. "Anne Murray Confident TV Special Will Be Ratings Hit." *Montreal Gazette*, October 1, 1989.

Nichols, Stephen. "Murray Much More than Just a Singer." *Calgary Herald*, October 22, 1991.

Oberbeck, S.K. "Barefoot Annie." *Newsweek*, June 24, 1974.

Ostick, Stephen. *Winnipeg Free Press*, November 25, 1989.

Penfield, Wilder. "Anne: Something To Talk About." Publication, Date, Page #.

Roura, Phil. "Anne Gives Capitol the Boot." *Calgary Herald*, May 8, 1992.

Smith, Jim. "What Ever Happened to Anne Murray?" *Sound*, 1980.

Stambler, Irwin & Landon, Grelan. *Encyclopedia of Folk, Country & Western Music*, 2nd Edition. New York: St. Martin's Press, 1984. pp. 490-493.

Steed, Judy. "Snowbird Anne Still All Business after 25 Years." *Toronto Star*, March 20, 1993.

Stern, Perry. "Anne Murray, The Secret of Her Success." *Canadian Musician*, 1990.

Sutton, Joan. "Cool as a Snowbird . . ." *Toronto Sun*, June 25, 1978, pp. S4.

Teitel, Jay. *Chatelaine*, May 1980. pp. 48, 125-134.

Thompson, Bob. "Showbiz Prince, Cancer Claims Anne Murray's Manager." *Toronto Sun*, April 1995.

✓ACKNOWLEDGEMENTS

There are, of course, some people to thank for their help or advice during the preparation of this book, but I promise to keep it brief.

In Springhill, Shelagh Rayworth and her staff at the Anne Murray Centre; David Farnell, for his assistance and economic advice, assorted members of the breakfast club for letting me eavesdrop and for keeping the coffee cup refilled. A special thank you to Kevin Cummings, manager of the Springhill and Parrsboro *Record* whose enthusiasm for the project exceeded expectations, as did his assistance.

At Quarry Press, Bob Hilderley, Susan Hannah, and others, not to mention Quarry writers John Einarson and Steve Ostick for their advice and encouragement, must also be thanked.

As promised, a helpful Pat McSweeney at *The Record*, yes dinner at Chez Piggy is still owed. A very special thanks to a beleaguered Larry LeBlanc, Canadian editor of *Billboard*, whose assistance went much beyond the call of duty and his passion for the music business.

Also acknowledged is the kind assistance of a wide variety of library soldiers, music pundits, and Anne Murray boosters.

This book is for my brother, Richard, a man who knows music so well and the business of it nearly as well. And it goes out to Sandra for her encouragement, patience, and understanding.